I receive many req
books of members, a
the time I decline d
volume of requests. It
write an endorsement for a couple I consider to be true
examples in the Body of Christ.

Today, there are millions of people living in turbulent
blended families as a result of remarriage. This story of
God working to bring the Houpe family to a place of
unity will keep you eager to continue reading.

Pastors Steve and Donna Houpe's testimony of God's
unmerited grace and their steadfast commitment to
family were instrumental in bringing about the changes
they desired for their family. It is through their submis-
sion and compassion, one to another, that the Houpe
family was able to receive God's promise.

The overwhelming success of Pastor Steve and Lady
Donna to bring their family to a place of agreement and
harmony confirms God's desire to perfect all that
concerns us. As they take you through their day-to-day
adventures in *Becoming One Family,* you will be
impacted and inspired to conquer your own journey.

You will learn how they continued to stand in faith
until they arrived at a place of victory. When you look at
the Houpe family today, you see the glory of God show-
cased to an unbelieving world.

It is sometimes very difficult to see and understand the
transformation involved in a caterpillar becoming a
butterfly. It is that unwavering, unconditional consistency
through the chrysalis stage that transforms an egg into a

beautiful, colorful butterfly of brilliance to impress all who see it. Get ready to be completely immersed as you read through their story in this well-written page-turner.

There is always a desire to send a message of hope to others still struggling with the challenge you have overcome. This book is that message of hope that will be the lifeline to so many who want better, but will only believe through the testimony of those who have been through it.

Enough of my commentary. You are about to be blessed as you begin reading their story. I know the Spirit of God will see that this message of hope gets into the right hands at the right time. Pastor Steve, Lady Donna, and the entire Houpe Family: thank you for allowing God to use your experiences with Him to make the story of His love and grace come alive.

Dr. Bridget Hilliard
New Light Christian Center Church
Houston, Texas

BECOMING ONE FAMILY:

Bringing Blended Families Together

By
Steve and Donna Houpe

Harrison House
Tulsa, Oklahoma

12 11 10 09   10 9 8 7 6 5 4 3 2 1

Becoming One Family:
Bringing Blended Families Together
ISBN 13: 978-1-57794-930-5
ISBN 10: 1-57794-930-7
Copyright © 2008 by Steve and Donna Houpe
P.O. Box 33903
Kansas City, MO 64120
Abridgeofhope@aol.com

Published by Harrison House Publishers, Inc.
P.O. Box 35035
Tulsa, Oklahoma 74135
www.harrisonhouse.com

Contents

DEDICATION

I dedicate this book believing that it contains vital truths for the health of the blended family. As I reflect over the years of rearing my children and taking care of my daily responsibilities, I would like to dedicate this work to my wife, Donna Leah, for your unqualified love and support.

I am who I am today because of you, and your protective concern personifies the Spirit of God's ability to help make us better.

I respect, rely on, and cherish you and our family—Stephen, Justin, Benjamin, Darell, Christa, Jonathan, and Penni!

ACKNOWLEDGMENT

We would like to acknowledge the team that labored with us tirelessly to bring this book into publication. Thank you for your support, encouragement, and prayers as you have witnessed and experienced our many bridge crossings.

FOREWORD

BY T. D. JAKES

I have spoken at Harvest Church. However, long before seeing it for the first time, I had heard about their fine, state-of-the-art facilities and the even-more-progressive vision the couple had.

The church was once a sprawling mall filled with various stores and huge corridors that now create the feeling of a conference center as opposed to its previous life as a shopper's delightful destination. Who, you might ask, was the one who renovated, almost reincarnated, the building and resurrected it—breathing into it a life-giving church, educational facility, and beautiful sanctuary filled with progressive break-out rooms? Who is the one that built what has become a spiritual destination for many who make pilgrimages from across the country to attend a conference or a teaching seminar? Or who was it that transformed the mall into a message so that many people from the greater Kansas area call this their spiritual home and place of worship? I am proud to say that all this was done by none other than the illustrious Dr. Steve Houpe—and, of course, he had quite a bit of help from his God!

Dr. Houpe and his wife, Donna, in spite of their massive accomplishments and extensive and diverse congregants, have maintained a humble persona—especially as people who have against all odds attained such status. They are neither unduly pompous, nor arrogant. They have the gift of being confident without going overboard into the extension of being arrogant. Together they are the perfect blend of "nice" and "spice" to make them the kind of people many fall helplessly in love with.

Anyway, I marveled as I sat on the stage waiting to speak as Steve and Donna (as I like to call them) moved around the stage, giving guidance and instruction, looking a little like a middle-aged, black version of Barbie and Ken. It is obvious that they have a synergy and comfortableness that most couples aspire to, but not all attain. As I through the years have come to know them, I have been shocked to learn that this pristine and polished-looking couple didn't get to where they are without some challenges along the way. Or as Langston Hughes so eloquently wrote, "Life for me ain't been no crystal stairs." I learned it hadn't been for them either. They went through many twists and turns along the way before they earned the right to guide others to the light of God's presence and the peace of a practical, pragmatic gospel—a gospel that now attracts thousands to that spiritual oasis they call church.

I realize that not everyone can or will have the luxury to know them personally—in part, because most public figures shield themselves from the onslaught of overexposure and crave privacy with the few quiet moments that they can sequester as their own. Perhaps that is why

I am so awed that people who have so little of their own privacy would sacrifice more of themselves to help others. I can only imagine that this current work, *Becoming One Family,* is just further evidence of the incredible way these two sacrifice themselves as public servants, not only of the Lord but also of His people.

So then, as my good friends Dr. Steve and Donna Houpe bare their souls to share that they were not always the family that they are today...as they openly and transparently share what they learned from a life that took turns going up the stairs and twists behind the scenes...read intently. They will discuss the taboo subjects of human frailties and failed marriages, and the bright future and hope that come from newfound love and a second chance at life. They go further than a love story of how two hurting people who found each other and were married in spite of public light and scrutiny survived. This is far less romantic than that, and yet much more practical. They don't teach us how one person marries another person. Instead, they leave us understanding how one family intertwines with another while children are in the middle of their lives, amidst busy schedules at church, and homework due in the morning. They lead us through the task of blending tight schedules of adolescent children with soccer practices, recitals, and countless others tasks and trials. Ultimately they share with us how they can give principles that will in the end become a tightly knitted composite of love and hope.

Like two Fortune 500 companies merging to form one entity, they show us the "behind the scenes" understanding we need—not only for those who have been given a similar challenge but to those of us who often need to counsel couples and give wisdom to families who face such things. The blended family is not something that happens outside of the church doors. It often happens for various reasons while we are attempting to live out our faith. And in many cases, families, through various circumstances, united before they came to church and need tips to make the merger more effective and congruent.

Inside this book you will learn how to use your faith and fervor to unlock a new love and build a new team in your house, even when it is built on the ashes of past relationships!

It is my good pleasure to introduce to some and present to others the wisdom, the logic, and the insight of two very fine people who not only married each other but also married each other's children and then taught the children to be coupled with each other. Get ready to throw rice as you read; and perhaps deeper still, get ready to glean something you and I can use in our lives as we go up and down the rugged stairways of a life that often twists and turns without warning!

Bishop T. D. Jakes, Sr.
The Potter's House
Dallas, Texas

PREFACE

In the spring of 2002, we had the privilege of visiting with one of my spiritual fathers, Dr. Leroy Thompson. This venture afforded my entire family an opportunity to sit at the feet of an incredible teacher, preacher, and prophet.

Our lives were tremendously changed as revelation from God poured into us from Heaven. For the very first time in our marriage, we felt simply compelled to take a closer look at our family—our blended family.

We have been involved in a blended family for over twenty years, and our objective is to share a bit of insight concerning some foundational principles, spiritual advice, and practical techniques in marriage. We have discovered that blending a family and keeping a sound mind in the process is very close to a miracle from God.

This journal of our experiences, failures, and victories will privilege you and your family to tour the home, the marriage, the family, and the journey of Steve and Donna Houpe. Our prayer is that you, your spouse, and most importantly, your children will be better equipped to enter into covenant with the Heavenly Father and with each other.

Our Prayer

Father, in the Name of Jesus, we thank You in advance for every blended family that will read this journey of our experiences. Our prayer is that You will reveal to each family Your plan and Your will for bringing each of them together. Lord, make plain Your complete vision to the husband of each household and confirm Your plan through the wife.

Prepare and equip each child involved to embrace Your will for their lives and to see the benefits of knowing those You have surrounding them. Father, we know that nothing is too hard for You. Therefore, we dedicate this book in honor of each blended family. Lord, keep them seeking You daily for direction, correction, and strength, in the wonderful Name of Jesus. Amen.

Now let's journey together through *Becoming One Family.*

Steve and Donna

INTRODUCTION

Let us begin by introducing our family to you. My wife, Donna, and I were both married and divorced before we met. Donna's marriage lasted a little over two years and she had one son, Darell, and was also raising her niece, Penni. My marriage lasted for ten years and to that union Justin, Benjamin, and Christa were born. However, prior to this marriage I had a son, born out of wedlock, who today is an adult, married, and raising his own blended family. His name is Stephen. I was so privileged to be a part of his life on a regular basis during his first few years; however, my times with him after the age of three were limited and less frequent. Our time together consisted of three to six visits a year and some long summers. Finally, after Donna and I were united in marriage, Jonathan was born. The ages of our children now range from ten to twenty-six. Four of them are adults.

There is one partner that must be present in stepfamilies from the very beginning—the power of God.

Our definition of a family agrees with the Holy Bible's description of the family—especially in Genesis, chapters one, two, and three, but generally throughout the entire book of Genesis.

The modern-day definition of the family as an alternative lifestyle is not what we promote or agree with. We truly stand on the aforementioned biblical description of marriage—that is, the union between a man and a woman. Thus, a blended family in our opinion is one in which either the husband (male gender) or the wife (female gender), or both, have children prior to uniting in marriage.

When our marriage began, my wife brought Darell, who then was six. Penni joined the family later, after she completed college. As for my children, Stephen was thirteen years old, Justin was nine, Benjamin was eight, and Christa was six. Once we had Jonathan and there were eight of us—and eventually nine with Penni—truthfully we had something very close to the "Brady Bunch," but our family was not at all like the classic story of *Cinderella*.

There will always be steps you can take toward unity in your blended family, and you will make it— one step at a time!

Stepfamilies are becoming a common part of the American fabric, and many in this nation's culture encounter their perils. Stepfamilies are facing bouts of confusion, suicidal and runaway children, the all-too-common silent partner of child molestation, high school dropouts, and juvenile delinquency. However, there is one partner that must be present in stepfamilies from the very beginning to bring supernatural healing to all who may hurt or be hurt by this union. That partner is the power of God. To speed up the seating during most restaurant visits early in our marriage, our family opted to eat at two separate tables of four close together instead of waiting for a table for eight. We soon discovered that with four growing boys (Jonathan had not yet been born) we needed to frequent restaurants that offered a buffet. It was the only place where the boys truly got full. One of the tasks we had to be the most creative about was the job of feeding our family.

Well, there you have it. This is our blended family, and welcome to our world! Our goal as we journey together through this book is to celebrate your union and encourage you through the hard times and the storms of life. We have attempted to address the structure of a family and discuss the importance of getting a vision from God. We have tried to describe the hurts and pains of divorce and its effects on the children. We have also noted the importance of preparing a new nest and dealing with weekend visits.

In addition, we have provided some necessary steps in the process of remarriage and understanding God's plan for the family. We are not declaring that we are the final authority on the subject of the blended family. Rather, our desire is simply to put you and your family at ease and encourage you to know that you are not alone and that you will make it. We are attempting to show that the pains of blending a family are real and that they subside for a while and can reoccur at the drop of a hat. Each time they surface, they lead your family another step closer to becoming one. Those pains can come during a birthday party where both biological parents and a step-parent are present, or when choosing whose game to attend, or by running out of film on the wrong child. Remember, there will always be steps you can take toward unity in your blended family, and you *will* make it—one step at a time!

We came to two vitally important conclusions, and we strongly emphasize them in this book:

1. You must understand the importance of allowing God to choose your mate and the need for preparing your children for remarriage.

2. Entering into a blended family is a very serious step for two people and it should not be taken lightly.

There are two reasons why we make these statements: First, when a blended family forms, a child is faced with the reality that the relationship between his or her biological parents failed. Second, the child is forced to accept a new parent.

Please understand—this decision to marry made by two adults and then dumped on innocent children is not as easy for the children to handle as many people have come to think. This is true even though half of marriages today have created blended families. Yet few couples are prepared to face the obstacles of a blended family.

Becoming One Family will dispel some of the untruths about blended marriages and encourage all families to believe that nothing is too hard for God and that your family will make it!

1

WILL YOUR FAMILY PROSPER OR PERISH?

1

WILL YOUR FAMILY PROSPER OR PERISH?

Where does it all begin—that is, the blended family? In the initial stages of our marriage, my wife always found herself answering the same old question: "Did you really give birth to six children?" Having to always describe our family structure, we immediately became sensitive to being different from many other families. One thing or another always reminded us that we were a blended family. We felt a silent pressure to explain our situation. But guess what? We finally wised up and discovered that we could respond to questions by saying, "Together, we have six children." This answer always left people

We knew that the deck was stacked against us, but we had God's promise that with Him, all things are possible.

speechless, and that was just what we wanted...no more questions about our family! From the beginning, we agreed not to acknowledge our children as stepchildren nor either of us as stepparents.

It was not long before we realized that our family was unique. Because our family was not structured according to God's original plan, we knew that our approach to parenting could not be traditional or conventional. Going into the marriage, we realized that we had only one competitive edge: if our marriage was going to succeed, we had to stand on the promises of God. We knew beyond the shadow of a doubt that the deck was stacked against us, but we had God's promise that with Him, all things are possible (see Matt. 19:26). We had to rely on, cling to, and stand on that very fact. We had to believe that *"I have strength for all things in Christ Who empowers me [I am ready for anything and equal to anything through Him Who infuses inner strength into me; I am self-sufficient in Christ's sufficiency]"* (Phil. 4:13 AMP).

WHAT IS YOUR FAMILY'S VISION?

Where do we begin? We have discovered that it all begins with a vision for the family. Over the past few months, we have thought a lot about our family's vision. Perhaps you are familiar with the scripture that declares,

"Where there is no vision, the people [or family] *perish"* (Prov. 29:18). My wife, Donna, brought this thought to the surface by asking me a very sobering question: *"Baby, what is our family's vision?"* Therefore we ask you, what vision has God given to *your* family? Are you and your family going in circles? Where are you going? What is your destination?

Let's look at several definitions of the word *vision.* One definition is, "something supposedly seen by other than normal sight; something perceived in a dream, trance, etc. or supernaturally revealed, as to a prophet." A vision can also be "the experience of having such a perception or revelation."[1] However, a vision is also God's idea revealed to man.

We can simplify this definition for the purposes of this book by saying that a vision is God's idea for a family revealed in a dream, a trance, or otherwise supernaturally. Thus, the vision for your family as well as ours must come from God.

As Donna and I began to reflect upon each of our families prior to marrying each other, we discovered something very crucial to our union—we lacked a vision. Through a very simple investigation, we discovered that every generation, on both sides of our families, had to start over again to achieve success. No foundation was laid for either of us to build upon, and no path was paved. There weren't any inheritances or businesses passed on to either of us or to our siblings. There were no special meetings held to read our parents' last will and testament.

LOOK FOR THE INHERITANCE

Getting a high school education was the starting point for each generation. Attending college was a goal embraced in the 1960s, and graduation from any university was celebrated by the family. However, the college grads in our families were few and far between, thus forcing each generation to start over again. Life became a never-ending marathon for the members of our families. No path was pioneered for the family to follow and no trail was blazed for the next generation. Each generation began its race from the runners' starting blocks after achieving a high school education or a college degree.

Donna and I decided that this cycle of "going nowhere" would end with our union. Satan's pattern of destruction in our family was over!

As Donna and I looked at both of our family structures, we discovered that our great-grandfathers all were poor, but all of them were hard workers. Our grandfathers were also poor, which left our fathers in poverty. Therefore, we concluded that unless we did something to change the legacy that was left to us, our own children would head down Poverty Boulevard like their ancestors.

IDENTIFY THE PATTERN OF DESTRUCTION

The pattern of poverty and divorce was handed down in my wife's family. That is to say, just as my wife's mother ended up divorced and raising two girls as a single mother, my wife ultimately also found herself divorced and a single mother raising a son alone. Additionally, my own divorce separated me from my children. Finally, as we joined in matrimony, we both declared, "Enough is enough!"

That is when Donna and I decided that this cycle of "going nowhere" would end with our union. Satan's pattern of destruction in our family was over! That's when our pursuit of God's true plan for our lives began. At that point, we decided and declared that our marriage would bring about a drastic change for our children and their children. We were determined to change the history of our family through our union. We decided that our family would begin to prosper and not perish!

2

A Promise Is
a Promise

2

A Promise Is a Promise

Let's take this time to reflect upon the story of Abraham and Sarah as recounted in Genesis, chapters 12 through 24. We are reminded that God came into covenant with them, and He gave Abraham a vision. As we saw in chapter 1, a vision is simply God's idea revealed to man.

In this promise or covenant that God made with Abraham, He required Abraham to leave his kindred (his siblings and extended family) and start a new life. God sent him into an unfamiliar land, far away from everyone he knew. But in this covenant, God promised to prosper Abraham and make him a father of many nations. Abraham was one hundred years old, and Sarah was ninety, when the Lord told him that Sarah would bear him a son (see Gen. 17:17). With Abraham and Sarah being that old, becoming a father and mother

Your immediate responsibility is to go before God in prayer and seek the vision that He has in store for you and your entire household.

presented its own share of unanswered questions. This was truly a dilemma for the two of them.

The questions they raised were: How is God going to do this for us in our old age? How is Abraham going to be the father of many nations without a child? Clearly, their advanced ages raised even more questions. I am sure that you would have asked the same ones! But as the story closes, God's promise to Abraham and Sarah was manifested through the birth and life of their son Isaac.

ANSWER THE CALL

Just as God called Abraham out from all that he knew, God is calling your family out to fulfill His vision in the earth realm today. You have been created for a plan that only God knows. Your family has been brought together to accomplish the task that lies ahead. You are equipped to execute, complete, and carry out God's plan for your life. Your immediate responsibility is to go before God in prayer and seek the vision that He has in store for you and your entire household.

YOU ARE A FAMILY WITH A VISION

What we love the most about the story of Abraham and Sarah is, it shows that God is all-knowing and almighty in impossible situations. We can all agree that this couple needed a miracle to bring to pass the will of the Father. And today we have come to learn how the miracle that took place in the lives of this couple has affected our world. That miracle has had a profound effect on every generation born since God made a covenant with Abraham.

The story of Abraham and Sarah shows us that God had a vision—a divine plan—for Abraham. Since God is no respecter of persons (see Acts 10:34), He has a divine plan for your family as well. Your responsibility is to seek God's face daily through prayer for His divine plan and purpose for your union. Your personal solicitation of the supernatural plan of God will place your family on the proper road to multiple blessings that will pass from generation to generation. Your pursuit of that plan must be with a pure heart as you embrace the will of God. Then sit back and watch the miracle that God will manifest in your life! You will have become not only a blended family, but a family with a vision from God! Congratulations!

3

GETTING A VISION FOR MY FAMILY

3

GETTING A VISION
FOR MY FAMILY

I believe we can all agree that the family is in desperate need of restoration. With the fragmentation of the traditional family and the lack of fathers in the home, coupled with increasing numbers of common-law marriages and same-sex marriages, we can easily conclude that we need help! As divorce rates rise in our society and the number of single-parent families increases, statistics have shown that the blended family is becoming increasingly common. One in three Americans is now a stepparent, stepchild, stepsibling, or some other member of a stepfamily.[1]

When we look back at God's original intent in creating the family through

God is interested in blessing you, your children, and your children's children, for generations.

the lives of Adam and Eve, we can acknowledge that He had a plan and purpose for the union of the man and woman. Today, we are responsible to inquire of God concerning His vision and plan for the success of our families. Because our blended families are not going away, we must commit our families to daily seek God's plan and direction for our households.

Know that God's plan for you and your family is designed to filter down to the generations to come. The blessings of God usually extend beyond your immediate union. That is, God is interested in blessing you, your children, and your children's children for generations.

What are we talking about? Well, do you recall Satan's pattern of destruction in families that we discussed in a previous chapter? We described the poverty, divorces, and single-parent families that recurred from generation to generation in both of our families. We talked about how we identified the destruction and chose to stop the madness, beginning with our union. If Satan's plan was for curses to pass from one generation to the next, then God's plan must be for blessings to be handed down from parent to child. Plainly said, we are speaking of generational blessings that God the Father wants to bestow upon His children and the generations to come.

DESIRE GOD'S WILL FOR YOUR FAMILY

The family vision that we speak of will come only from God and can be birthed only out of prayer and consecration before Him. In the next few days, gather your family together and seek the face of God for His plan and purpose for your life and the lives of your children. Desire God's will and pray at least three times a day. God will not disappoint you as you seek Him with a pure and sincere heart.

STOP THE CYCLE OF DESTRUCTION

Today we must stop the cycle of lack, poverty, depression, loneliness, divorce, sickness, child abuse, and anything else that has plagued our families for generations. We must declare that generational blessings are on the way for each of our families. Our prosperity is directly related to the plan that God reveals to each of us. We must become families with vision, thereby avoiding the likelihood of perishing.

Your success in rearing your blended family is wrapped up in your yes to the will of the Father.

As we follow the story of Abraham and Sarah, we discover that Abraham's assignment from God required the handiwork of God in order to come to pass. It is the same for you and us. In the case of blended families, we must grasp that we cannot expect to achieve success without the leading of God—the Father of Abraham, Isaac, and Jacob.

Our hope and trust must be in Him, and we must rely upon Him. Our confidence must rest in the knowledge that God brought us together to fulfill His plan.

Will you say yes to your assignment? Your spouse is waiting on you. God is waiting on you. Most importantly, your innocent children are waiting on your answer. Your success in rearing your blended family is wrapped up in your yes to the will of the Father. The choice is now before you. Your yes to God's plan for you and your blended family is a big step toward making your family one.

Let's Pray

Father, in the Name of Jesus, we say yes to Your divine plan for our family. We, the _____ (Insert your family's name.) family, submit our wills to Your will as we seek You both day and night. Lord, show us Your plan and purpose for our union. We trust You to bring every component of Your plan to life in us. Amen.

Family Exercises

1. Decide on a special time for the family to pray. Seek God's face for His plan and His will. Pray until you get an answer from God.

2. Write down the vision so that everyone will know what it is.

3. Discuss your family's vision with your spouse first.

4. Call a family meeting, and thoroughly discuss the vision with the entire family.

5. Allow for questions, comments, and remarks before closing the meeting.

6. Speak over the vision daily and declare that it shall come to pass in the Name of Jesus.

7. Never allow yourself to lose sight of the vision. Remind yourself, your spouse, and the children of what God has spoken.

SCRIPTURE REFERENCES

Isaiah 29:11

Habakkuk 2:2

4

WHERE DID IT

GO WRONG?

4
WHERE DID IT GO WRONG?

STEVE:

Before I knew it, I found myself curled up in a blanket in my basement, alone and in the dark. No longer did I hear the sound of my children's feet as they raced through the kitchen. Facing a divorce and looking at the destruction of the family, I resorted to something I used to do in my childhood—sit in the dark alone. The sound that my ears had grown so accustomed to hearing was no longer to be heard. Where were they? How were they doing? How did I end up here?

DONNA:

It was the middle of the night and I found myself packing and loading up my car. Was this really

Many of us didn't choose a mate based upon the Word of God. Our choice was formulated and based upon Hollywood's depiction of love.

happening to me? I was certain that I could not go on any longer. My final episode found me swiftly stuffing my things into large black garbage bags, packing my baby's toys in clothes baskets, and putting my dog in the back of the truck. I needed to just "get out of Dodge"! Going where—back to my mother's house and my old bedroom, with my baby tucked in beside me. I rehearsed it over and over again...how did I end up back here?

CHOOSING A MATE

There are so many divorces today simply because we are not following God's original plan, even on how to choose a mate. Many of us didn't choose a mate based upon the Word of God. Our choice was formulated and based upon Hollywood's depiction of love. Statistics have even shown that more than 77 percent of Americans are choosing to cohabit after the first marriage in situations involving no children, and more than 63 percent cohabit in relationships involving two or more children.[1] Many factors contribute to the increase in cohabitation after divorce in the American culture. The statistics are alarming in that they show that a large number of children are forced to live in homes where the adults have chosen to live together but not marry.

Please note: Trying to blend a family without the blessing of God on your life means there are many difficult roadblocks ahead for you and your family.

Outward appearances and the need for self-fulfillment are often prominent forces in what prompt people to choose whom they will marry. This must be said: a person's outward

Many good men and women would make wonderful husbands and wives, if someone would just look into their hearts.

appearance does not reveal who that person is inside.

Many good men and women would make wonderful husbands and wives, if someone would just look into their hearts. Unfortunately, physical appearance bears far too much weight in the decision for many people. Many men seem to think, *If she's pretty, she's a good woman.* Many women seem to think, *If he's handsome, he's a good man. If he's rich, he will be a good provider. If he is strong physically, he will protect me.* Not allowing God to guide you in choosing the right mate will lead you into deception, false hopes, and delusions of what your marriage should be.

Today at least one third of all children are expected to live in a stepfamily before they reach the age of 18. The blended family is becoming more the norm than an

God sees the whole thing, and only He can fix it!

aberration. Because stepfamilies are so complicated, it takes a long time—often four to seven years, or longer—for people to get to know each other, create positive relationships, and develop a family history.

RECOGNIZE THE ATTACK

The devil attacks the family because the family affects all of society. The majority of societal problems in the world stem from problems in the family, such as incest, physical abuse, alcoholism, poverty, infidelity, pornography, homosexuality, single-parent households, and high school-dropout rates, to name only a few.

The church has not openly addressed these issues, but they are now being forced into the forefront for discussion by changes in contemporary culture. Over fifty percent of people in Christian church congregations in the USA are in, or related to, a blended family. Conservative statistics show that the divorce rate for remarriages exceeds sixty percent. Part of the reason for this high rate is that most struggling stepfamilies dissolve and end in divorce within the first four years—before their family has had time to blend.

In years past, troubling issues such as this were not discussed. However, we cannot afford the luxury of ignorance or the ease of silence concerning such matters. *The purpose and protection of our families are at stake!*

When you are in a divorce situation, you are forced to seek God for His plans and not your own. Divorce is a process that brings pain, confusion, bitterness, rejection, and sometimes resentment. God sees the whole thing, and only He can fix it! He can and will restore, repair, and replace everything that was destroyed in your life. Now, embrace His plan and purpose for your life!

Let's Pray

Dear Lord, I thank You that Your hand is still upon me, even in this most difficult time. I surrender my thoughts and my plans to You. Do with them what You will. Protect my children from any hurt and harm, and make clear Your purpose for my family, in Jesus' Name. Amen.

Family Exercises

1. Pray: Jeremiah 29:11 NLT. Seek the plan of God for your life.

   Father God, Your Word says that You know the plans You have for me and my family—plans for good and not for disaster, to give us a future and a hope.

2. Forgive yourself for all the wrong choices you have made.

3. Pray for all the children involved.

4. Begin preparing your heart to love again.

5. Purpose in your heart to stay in this new marriage.

SCRIPTURE REFERENCES

Matthew 6:33,34

Genesis 2:18, 21–23

5

FORGIVE, FORGET, AND MOVE ON

5

FORGIVE, FORGET, AND MOVE ON

My wife and I have both experienced a divorce, and we discovered that many divorcees go through seven stages following the divorce or the ending of a relationship. These are: denial, reconciliation, depression, letting go, forgiveness, reclaiming your world, and celebration. Little did we know that successfully walking through and out of each of these stages prepared us to move on and helped create our pathway to one another.

We want to take this time to personally share each stage with you. Perhaps you have experienced a divorce or the ending of a relationship, and you will see yourself at one of these stages. If you do, note this: how long you linger

Letting go and moving on from the relationship can be extremely difficult.

at one or all of these stages totally depends on you. Now allow us to share these seven stages with you.

DENIAL

You may find yourself thinking, *I can't believe this is happening to me. I didn't get married so that I could become divorced. When I said, "I do," I said, "for better or for worse." I said, "until death do us part." I thought we would be together forever.* The very first stage is denial. A number of emotional changes happen during this time.

During the denial stage, a person doesn't want to face the fact that the relationship is over. This can be a very emotional time. Letting go and moving on from the relationship can be extremely difficult. One thing people find themselves doing during this stage is talking to anyone who will listen. But the One you should talk to is God.

How do you recover from the stage of denial? Donna and I recovered by going to God's Word and trusting that He knows the thoughts and plans He has for our lives—plans of hope, to give us a future (see Jer. 29:11). He also promised in His Word that He would never leave us nor forsake us (see Heb. 13:5). His promises are true for you. Remember that you are not alone—God is with you.

Depression can come in many forms.

RECONCILIATION

"Are we ever going to get back together?" It is possible to reconcile after divorce. Sometimes it does happen. But even though one person can start the process of reconciliation, two people must be in agreement in order for it to come to pass. Both parties must be willing to start the love walk again.

How can reconciliation take place? It is possible when both of you begin to acknowledge the problems you had in the past, and then you make a concerted effort to work together. My wife and I discovered that reconciliation cannot take place without two people first confessing their failures to one another, maintaining open discussions, forgiving, and then moving on.

DEPRESSION

"I just don't feel like getting up today. I don't seem to have any energy to do anything." If those words express how you feel, you have entered into the stage of depression. Depression can come in many forms. It can attack your body in such a way that a pattern of destruction can develop in the form of ulcers, hair loss, weight loss or gain, lethargy, and other ailments. Life can become unbalanced when the spirit of depression is present.

DONNA:

You can wallow in any of these stages as long as you want to, but when you have had enough, the power of God is readily available to get you out.

I experienced a physical breakdown and was forced to deal with some real emotional issues during the stages of my separation and divorce. If it had not been for the immediate help of my family and my pastor, Dr. Leroy Thompson of Darrow, Louisiana, I would not have made it, and you would not be reading this book.

I found myself deep in debt, physically ill, emotionally a wreck, and of no assistance to my ten-month-old son. I could not even afford to purchase diapers, formula, or other food for him. Even though I was a middle school teacher with a master's degree, my salary was spent before I received it. I am forever thankful for my mother, my sisters, and their girls as they rallied around me and became my immediate support system. The Word of God strengthened me on the inside, and after three years I found myself ready to love again.

HOPELESSNESS

Hopelessness may surface during this time. You may experience grief because you find yourself alone. Hopelessness can bring the spirit of suicide, but this will not happen to you. At this point, you must find something in your life that will cause you to want to live. Your desire to move on must overpower the desire to stay in a rut. Remember: you can wallow in any of these stages as long as you want to, but when you have had enough, the power of God is readily available to get you out. It's up to you.

Our suggestion is for you to rise up, get out, and do something! Take your life back!

DONNA:

I tell this story often because I believe that I am alive to tell it only because of the little spark of inspiration God placed in my life. As I lay on my back in Our Lady of the Lake Hospital following the separation—my body no longer able to function—my sister, Lorraine, entered the room with my son, Darell. He was only ten months old and had just started to walk. As he reached for me, a spark of life hit my body, and I found myself thinking that no one would raise him but me. On that day, I purposed in my heart that I had to live for him and I must be strong for him. Darell became my reason to live. Seven days later, I was back at my mother's home on the three-month road to recovery.

Our suggestion is for you to rise up, get out, and do something! Take your life back! How can you do this?

Forgetting is a critical component of forgiveness.

Read Psalm 38. God's Word will inspire you, strengthen you, and empower you. Identify your support system, depend upon the Word of God, and allow the healing process to begin.

LETTING GO

"How do I pull myself together and move on from here?" When you are ready to release all unhealthy connections from your past, you are in the position to let go. If anything makes you feel bad or upsets you, *let it go!*

We once heard a great man of God, Dr. Roy Hicks, say that when you talk about something in your past that was not positive, you pick it up and place it in front of you. This causes you to have to plow through it again. What's in the past, leave in the past! It was of no benefit to you then. It probably will not benefit you now, so leave it back there! Forgive, forget, and move on!

Know that God is equipping and preparing you for greatness. Your life is not over and your time is not done. Now begin to identify your strengths and weaknesses. Go for the gusto! Step out of your comfort zone and try something new. Start creating new memories and experiences and building new godly relationships. Let your conversations be ones of hope and inspiration, and do not allow past hurts to drag you back into the underbrush of pain. Remember, if you allow it, you will be forced to plow through that pain again and again. Suggestion: pack up the plow, or sell it and get a new start!

*You **must** forget before you can successfully move on.*

FORGIVENESS

You may find yourself thinking, *I'll forgive them, but I won't forget.* Let's examine this thought closely. Forgetting is a critical component of forgiveness. In forgiving, you must pardon the one who hurt you and refuse to be a slave to your past. Choosing to hold on to the hurt, disappointment, and rejection will only keep you in bondage. Once you climb this mountain of forgiveness, you *must* forget before you can successfully move on. Remember, God has forgiven you of your imperfections, and He expects you to forgive others. Now release yourself from unforgiveness so you can reclaim your world!

RECLAIMING YOUR WORLD

"Hello world, I'm back!" At this stage, your talk and walk are new. Your focus is on getting back on your feet, creating a new life void of the ex-spouse, and charting new territory along with your children. You are primed and ready to allow God to define your new world. He

Remember, God desires for you to prosper.

must be the core of your existence—at the center of your decisions, plans, and activities. Put your trust totally in Him. He can handle it!

CELEBRATE GOOD TIMES...COME ON!

The final stage is celebration. You have survived the seven stages of divorce and you are in a place where you are ready to enjoy living again. At this juncture, you are walking in total victory. Remember, God desires for you to prosper. Your abundant blessings lie in wait for you. Receiving all of God's best has everything to do with *you*. You are ready to say "I do" for the last time. Now let God do the choosing. Let Him form and fashion you for your new spouse, and he or she will fit you like a glove. You have now forgiven, forgotten, and moved on. Congratulations!

Let's Pray

Father, in the Name of Jesus I place this hurt before You. I cast this care upon You. Lord, help me to walk through these stages and receive total healing in every area. And, Lord, bless and keep my children as we walk through this season of our lives. Help them make adjustments for the things to come. Amen.

Family Exercises

1. Identify what stage you are in. (Be honest with yourself.)

2. Together as a family, read Psalm 38 and Psalm 91.

3. Set personal goals for reclaiming your world.

4. Write down five things you desire to do with the help and power of God.

5. Plan a celebration party. Invite three to five friends over and declare your victory.

6. Consider your budget and treat yourself and your children to a victory treat!

SCRIPTURE REFERENCES

Psalm 38

Psalm 91

Ephesians 4:32

6

THE ATTRACTION

6

THE ATTRACTION

Let's look at this hypothetical scenario: A single dad named Joe and his son, Anthony, comprise a household. One day, after being a single dad for a few years, Joe says, "You know, Lord, I think I'd like to get married again. I really don't want to spend the rest of my life alone." He then asks his son how he feels about his dad's desire to remarry. "Anthony, we've been by ourselves for a while now," he says. "You and I know that I haven't been the best housekeeper and I've burned many meals. The truth is, we could use a little help and I just don't want us to be by ourselves anymore. What do you think of the possibility of Dad remarrying?"

Speaking with your children, whether they live with you or not,

It is not a good idea to surprise your children with a new spouse, because if you do, they may surprise you with disagreement.

concerning your desire to remarry is an important step to take before moving into a new union. This is the beginning stage of planning for a successful blended family. Introduction to a new parent opens the window of imagination for all parties involved. The adults focus only on the love that they share; they rarely zero in on how their remarriage will impact the children. It is not a good idea to surprise your children with a new spouse, because if you do, they may surprise you with disagreement. Unfortunately, disagreement can come in many different forms in a new union.

As your children are being prepared for your remarriage, you will also need to prepare your extended family—your parents and siblings. By opening the lines of communication, you will set the stage for introducing a new person to your family. While you envision a new beginning for your life, you also need to help your loved ones transition into that new life by including them. You need to recognize that even though you went through the divorce physically and mentally, your family members also experienced a loss.

Remember during this preparation time that your family members genuinely love you. Though they may sometimes say things that hurt your feelings, that is most likely not their intention. Understand that this preparation period will help all of you walk in agreement, which will bring the blessings of God. Let God begin to minister to their hearts. It may not happen overnight, but in time, your family will get in agreement with your decision if their love for you is genuine and they desire to see you happy again.

SPIRITUAL ATTRACTION

"Okay, Lord, I'm ready for a new mate. Cute didn't work the first time. Now I want a godly mate!" Our question to you is, are you really ready for a godly mate?

WHO ARE YOU ATTRACTING?

If in your heart you desire a godly mate, you need to discover what God wants. Your first focus should be to attract God spiritually in all that you say or do. When you are attractive to God, you will attract a godly mate, because a godly mate wants someone who represents Christ.

When your marriage is founded on God's choice for you, His Word will keep you. You will find your children in a safe union and a nurturing environment where they will grow, and you will produce healthy children.

Everyone says they want a godly mate because it sounds good, it's biblically correct, and it makes everyone feel safe. However, even when a person claims to be looking for that kind of mate, he or she might go too far physically to try to attract someone, and yet remain spiritually unprepared. That person has emphasized the wrong aspect in preparing for a future husband or wife. There are still some unsafe people in the church that are willing to marry you. Beware!

THE NINETY-TEN RULE

Maybe you are giving ninety percent of your effort to preparing physically to attract the opposite sex and ten percent to preparing spiritually. By doing this, you hope to sustain the relationship. Baby, you are using the wrong bait. And you will get the same results as before. As you make the effort to prepare yourself spiritually and trust God to bring into your life the person who will benefit you and your children, your chances of divorce after remarriage will diminish considerably.

When your marriage is founded on God's choice for you, His Word will keep you. You will find your children in a safe union and a nurturing environment where they will grow, and you will produce healthy children. We know that the blended family is not God's original intent for families, but He is able to take our mess and turn it into a message. That's why you are reading this book today. We are simply presenting the story of our mess to encourage you to keep trusting God, because He is faithful.

FLIP THE NUMBERS

We said earlier that spending ninety percent of your effort on physical preparations and ten percent on the spiritual will yield the wrong results. However, you can flip the numbers. If a couple's relationship is ninety percent spiritually focused and ten percent physically focused, they will have a foundation for a spiritually strong marriage. Realize that being spiritually focused means being keenly aware of each other's spiritual condition. Regular church attendance is not a sure sign that he or she is a believer—a hearer and a doer of the Word of God.

SEEING IS NOT BELIEVING

What we are endeavoring to make clear to you is, when you are ready to consider a godly marriage, it is paramount that you look beyond the "Bible-toting, scripture-quoting, church-attending person." Ask God to reveal their true relationship with Him, and believe that He will show you. Seek the counsel of those who lead you spiritually and inquire about the individual's faithfulness. Trust those to whom you have submitted your spiritual life and that of your children, and use wisdom.

Now you are probably asking, "How will I know if the person has a relationship with God?" Our question to you is, "How is your relationship with God?" The Bible

Outward appearance is not lasting. What sustains a relationship is a whole, godly, caring person who is good on the inside.

says in Matthew 6:33,34, *"Seek first the kingdom of God and His righteousness, and all these things shall be added to you. Therefore do not worry about tomorrow, for tomorrow will worry about its own things. Sufficient for the day is its own trouble."*

You must first seek *God's* Kingdom and *His* righteousness, and *then* all of the things you desire will be given to you. When? When your first priority is the Kingdom of God and His righteousness. What you are seeking is His way of thinking, His way of doing things, and His direction daily. This means walking as Christ walked upon the earth and living in such a way that He is represented in all that you say and do. Sometimes we try to separate God from our Monday through Saturday lives. We need to seek God every day, not just on Sunday. When we do that, God will answer us and give us the desires of our heart.

PHYSICAL ATTRACTION

This is the area where most of us probably have the most practice. Preparing physically for a mate consumes the world around us every day. We are bombarded by the media, by billboards, on the job, in the malls, and simply by the people we meet on the street. Some people are professionals at preparing physically to face the world, and we have all been captivated by their beauty. But we have come to learn that outward appearance is not lasting. What sustains a relationship is a whole, godly, caring person who is good on the inside.

Seeking God about marriage does not erase the need to spend some time making necessary improvements to your natural life, such as to your appearance and finances. Perhaps you can incorporate certain disciplines such as diet and exercise that will improve your appearance. Treat yourself, your children, and your home to a makeover. You will be surprised how good it will make you feel. And if necessary, make adjustments to your spending habits. You should desire to bring your best to the table.

There is one final thing you must do to prepare for a new spouse. If you are rearing your children alone and you desire to remarry, you should present your family before God as something that is pleasing in His sight. What you tolerate from your children, no one else has to. That's not to say no one will, but no one else has to.

If you are tolerating any ungodly conduct in your children—such as disrespect to you, failing grades, or other unwanted behavior—you should not expect a new

God promises it will happen for you and your children, if you will seek Him and keep Him first.

marriage partner to tolerate it. Therefore, in your time of preparation for remarriage, begin to prepare your children as well as yourself. You should train them to obey not only the Lord but also to honor and respect you and others in authority.

DONNA:

In your planning and your prayer time, include your whole family. In my life, I have seen how beneficial this can be. Before Steve and I were married, I presented the idea of a new daddy to our son Darell. When he was about four years old, he returned from church and declared that our pastor said that he could ask God for anything he wanted. So that night as we bowed our knees for prayer, he said that he was going to pray and ask God for a new daddy. A few months passed and he came home one day and said, "Momma, I think I want to ask God for a house that has an upstairs."

We prayed in agreement, and he and I began to search the free home-buying magazines for our new house. As time went by, his prayers became more directed and stronger. After two years had passed, Darell said, "You know, Mom, I think I'm going to ask God for a big brother and a little sister."

Just before Darell turned six years old, my husband and I met. At that moment, Darell found the fulfillment of his vision and the answer to his prayers. There was a house with an upstairs, and he inherited three big brothers and a little sister.

This is a cherished life example of how God will give you the desires of your heart, if you will seek Him first. Every one of Darell's requests came to pass. God promises it will happen for you and your children, if you will seek Him and keep Him first.

Let's Pray

God, You alone are Lord, and I am so thankful that You are a part of my life. I thank You for this day and my family. God, I will seek Your face and Your Word today. Direct me in everything I say, do, and touch. I thank You, Lord, that You are fashioning and forming me for my mate, and my mate for me, in Jesus' Name. Amen.

Family Exercises

1. Identify what you and your children desire from God.

2. Determine what you would like to see in your family.

3. Begin a regular family prayer time.

4. Read the Book of Ruth.

5. Make necessary adjustments to your physical appearance.

6. Introduce the concept of remarriage to the children before you begin a new relationship.

7. Include your children in your decisions.

8. Pray daily for the wisdom of God.

SCRIPTURE REFERENCES

Matthew 6:33,34

Matthew 8:19

The Book of Ruth

Proverbs 3:5

7

CHOICES BRING CHANGES

7

CHOICES BRING CHANGES

The chairs have been placed in their familiar circle. We are all here. As we speak one by one, there is silence and intensity in the room, and the atmosphere is riddled with fear. Mom, being the analyzer, always speaks last. She captures the heart of the matter. Dad sits quietly with his Bible in his hand. He's thumbing through the pages looking for what God has to say. Who is it going to be this time? What is he going to say? When dad calls a meeting, he has something to say, and it is always backed by the Word of God. One thing is for certain—when he is finished, there will be some changes taking place in the house. When he speaks, his words are spoken with a

Change opens the door for different emotions and feelings that need to be addressed. As parents, we have to address them, and we have to respond with maturity even when it is difficult to do so.

sternness never heard before among those present.... "There will be no more hurt in this family. There has been enough hurt. Everybody living in this house is my child. Everyone living under my roof is equal. If you don't act right, you've got to go." Welcome to a typical Houpe family meeting.

ENTERING INTO A NEW MARRIAGE

Nearly every couple enters marriage with the hopes and dreams of happily ever after, but somewhere along the way choices bring changes. Those changes can strengthen, alter, or destroy the family unit. In any family situation, change is inevitable. However, in a blended family change happens regularly—much more often than God's intention for the original family structure. Change alters the familiar and, while it can be fun, it can also be scary or sad. Change opens the door for different emotions and feelings that need to be addressed. As parents, we have to address them, and we have to respond with maturity even when it is difficult to do so.

When we consider blending families, we must realize that some things have been broken and must undergo reconstruction. Jesus wants to know about our hurts and concerns, and He alone can bring wholeness to the blended family. Psalm 147:3 NIV tells us, *"He heals the brokenhearted and binds up their wounds."*

When a divorce occurs, there are always casualties. Both the parents and the children are wounded. When a remarriage occurs, those wounds do not automatically heal—especially in the children. The healing and reconstruction process takes time. Periodic family meetings like the one described above have been a stepping-stone to aid our family in becoming one.

STEVE:

We remember holding many family meetings—and holding them on a regular basis—because the children were not all living with us at the time, and their emotional health was important to us. We recall one particular family meeting we held at our cabin. This meeting went on for about two hours, and it revealed the hurts of all of the children. Justin and Benjamin in particular expressed the deep hurt they had felt as they approached their state championship football game. This meeting took place months after the game, and it surprised us that both of them were feeling the same pain. It was truly a time of ministry to our sons as we listened. However, the meeting brought about a release for both of them and we watched them become free from that hurt. We took another step toward becoming one family.

As the blended family works toward reconstruction, familiar family roles change.

My wife and I have attempted to remain sensitive to our children's feelings throughout the time of our union. We would ask each other, "How is Christa doing?" "What do you think Justin is feeling?" "Have you talked with Stephen lately?" "Where is Penni?"

SENSITIVITY IS VITAL

As the blended family works toward reconstruction, familiar family roles change. Change and the unfamiliar can trigger abnormal conduct in a child. In other words, the child may act in a way in which he or she would not normally behave. For example, a compliant child may suddenly become defiant.

My wife and I witnessed this type of reaction in one of our children when we married and blended our two families. After our marriage, one particular child shut down academically and lost interest in school. He was an honor-roll student in a private middle school. Learning came easily to him. He is brilliant and talented, and we are still working on trying to help him discover this.

As parents, we need to allow our children an adequate amount of time to adjust and heal.

He later wrote us a letter describing his pains, disappointments, and confusion. There was so much that he did not understand. He ended his letter with an apology as he repented before God for trying to inflict on us the same pain that he felt. His exact words were, "...because I was hurting, I wanted you to hurt." Remember: hurting people hurt people.

In this kind of situation, a parent might attempt to discipline the child, but that would not solve anything. The pain is too deep, the wounds are too fresh, and the hurt is not going away. The issue is deeper than that. Through prayer, consideration, and patience, the healing power of God can go to work. As parents, we need to allow our children an adequate amount of time to adjust and heal.

We must always bear in mind that the children did not divorce their parent. The children will need time to process the changes mentally and emotionally. We cannot discipline our children for something that will heal in time.

Periodically, I encouraged my wife to talk to our son Darell, who was born to her and her ex-husband. There was a possibility that he might have been hurting in an area that we were not familiar with, and he would not discuss it with me, but he would with her. If there was a problem, rather than allowing it to go unnoticed, we could deal with it.

Raising a family takes work, but blending families requires overtime!

TRUST YOUR GUT

In order to help you resolve problems that may arise in the family, ask the Holy Spirit to enlighten you. The Holy Spirit is that inner voice that speaks to us occasionally. Some psychologists may refer to this as your subconscious. You'll just know down in your spirit that something is wrong.

For example, one child may be teased by the other children. Words can be spoken in your absence that bring pain to another. Address the situation, defuse it, and do not tolerate it. Your family will face enough opposition outside of the home; therefore, you should have zero tolerance for any confusion within the home. In some instances, you may want to have a child's biological parent meet with him or her so that the child feels freer to share the truth. Otherwise, Daddy, it is time for you to address each issue and escort your family further down the road to becoming one. Remember: Raising a family takes work, but blending families requires overtime!

As we try to help our children heal, we ourselves need to heal. It takes a lot of time, diligence, and hard work. By allowing the healing power of God to begin to work in us as adults, we open the door for healing to begin in our children. Acknowledge that each child will deal with the divorce in his or her own time and way. This will keep things constantly changing until the hurt is gone and each child has walked through those seven stages of divorce just as the two of you have. When each one arrives at the destination of being ready to embrace the love of a step-parent, the family will move much closer to becoming one. Bringing a blended family together is a lifelong process that requires patience and understanding.

Let's Pray

Dear Lord, we thank You for our blended family, and we acknowledge that we have not made the best choices. But now we surrender our entire family to You. Keep our family close to You and guide us daily in all of our actions, decisions, and ways. Without Your guidance, we acknowledge that we would be lost. We thank You, Lord, for intervening in our family's plan and taking over, in Jesus' Name. Amen.

Family Exercises

1. Hold regular family meetings.

2. Husband and wife: spend time discussing the status of each child in the union.

3. Set aside a special time during which you and your spouse can express to each other your own fears and concerns.

4. Schedule a family prayer time to remind the family that you are trusting God for the victory in your family.

5. Schedule routine visits with schoolteachers, school counselors, youth ministers, coaches, and anyone else who has a direct or indirect impact on the lives of your children. These people are a part of your support system that God has surrounded you with. Do not ignore their influence and impact. You have help.

SCRIPTURE REFERENCES

Psalm 147:3

Isaiah 58:8

Proverbs 18:21

8

BUILDING A NEW NEST

8

BUILDING A NEW NEST

When a man and a woman take a vow to become husband and wife, they begin the process of building a new house—a new nest. On that day, the man and woman perhaps stand before a preacher and a select company of people and proceed to build their new nest together. Behind each of them lies a great history. But on that certain day, they publicly declare that they are building a new nest of their own.

When wisdom builds your house, riches fill it. Peace is in your living room, patience is in your kitchen, and hope is in your hallway.

For those who are making the second vow, old nests lie in the past. For these, issues from the old nest may begin to reside in the new nest. We are going to discover what it takes to build a new nest, no matter what your past may be like. The Bible says that every house is built by someone (see Heb. 3:4). We have a question for you. Who is building your house? In other words, who is leading in your house?

Building a new house or an old house, a new nest or an old nest, takes the same thing: wisdom. We see that in the Book of Proverbs: *"Through wisdom a house is built, and by understanding it is established; by knowledge the rooms are filled With all pleasant and precious riches"* (Prov. 24:3,4). Those precious and pleasant riches are the fruit of the Spirit: love, joy, peace, patience, kindness, goodness, faithfulness, gentleness, and self-control (see Gal. 5:22,23 NIV). When wisdom builds your house, riches fill it. Peace is in your living room, patience is in your kitchen, and hope is in your hallway.

WHAT DOES IT TAKE TO BUILD AGAIN?

Proverbs 24:3,4 in *The Living Bible* says, *"Any enterprise is built by wise planning, becomes strong through common sense, and profits wonderfully by keeping abreast of the facts."* This is why we need to gain knowledge and wisdom. We need to look deeper into the Word so we can walk in greater wisdom concerning our homes, our nests, for they are built on the wisdom of God. James 1:5,6 tells us how we can gain this wisdom: *"If any of you lacks wisdom, let him ask of God, who gives to all liberally and without reproach, and it will be given to him. But let him ask in faith, with no doubting, for he who doubts is like a wave of the sea driven and tossed by the wind."*

When we ask for wisdom, we are to ask in faith. Then God will reveal things to us and we will not be tossed to and fro by doubt. God will give us the wisdom we ask for, but it won't always be what we expect.

Have you ever witnessed a bird building a nest for her young? It is a fascinating experience. One time a bird was building a nest on the sill of our laundry room window. We saw the mother bird bringing twigs and dirt to build a safe haven for her babies. We then saw the eggs and how she watched and protected them ever so carefully from anything that could possibly harm them. As nature would permit, the eggs hatched and the birds flew away.

This process of nature reminds us of how two individuals with children must prayerfully and systematically come together to build a nest. They must build a nest where everyone feels protected and loved.

SEVEN KEY AREAS

There are seven key areas in which a family blends:

1. Spiritual things

2. Relationships

3. Finances

4. Primary Beliefs

5. Emotions

6. Family History

7. Life Span

SEVEN KEY AREAS TO CONSIDER
BEFORE BLENDING A FAMILY

1. SPIRITUALITY

Donna: You must take the time to observe the future spouse's spiritual family structure. Is this a Christian family or just a religious family? Is this a family that operates in faith? Is this a Spirit-led family that I am going to unite with? There was no doubt in my mind that my husband had a solid spiritual structure.

A couple contemplating marriage needs to make sure that they can live in agreement on a spiritual level.

Whatever the spiritual structure of each family, the union of marriage will join the structures together in building the new house. Therefore, it is important that each person spend adequate time identifying the other family's spiritual beliefs. God's wisdom on this matter is found in Matthew 7:24,25. Jesus said, *"Therefore whoever hears these sayings of Mine, and does them, I will liken him to a wise man who built his house on the rock: and the rain descended, the floods came, and the winds blew and beat on that house; and it did not fall, for it was founded on the rock."* So when the rains, storms, and floods come, your house will remain. In other words, when the bills, the bankruptcy, the challenges, the children's misbehavior, or sickness comes, your home will remain strong because it is built on the rock—the Word of God.

Therefore, a couple contemplating marriage needs to make sure that they can live in agreement on a spiritual level. They will have success when they build their new home on the Word of God.

2. RELATIONSHIPS

Before you say I do, observe what kind of relationship your future spouse's family has with one another. Statistics show that most women and men marry individuals who have similar traits as their parents. Find out the answers to these questions:

- Do the mother and father have a good relationship with your future mate?

- How is the relationship between the mother and father?

- Do the parents have good relationships with their children, and vice versa?

- What kind of relationship does the immediate family have with the extended family?

All of these relational issues are important. They need to be observed and discussed before two people blend their families and build a nest together. Doing so will help all of the people involved strengthen the new structure.

3. FINANCES

Money is one of the main issues that can destroy a marriage. The financial component is vital to any successful union. How financially stable is the family you are about to commit your life to? For example, if you have to keep loaning money to the same member, you have become their sponsor.

When you become a sponsor, you become financially responsible for whatever they are participating in. Sponsorship is not something most couples consider when they are starting out, especially if you are trying to blend a family. If you have to sponsor a member of your future spouse's family every time the family needs to go on a trip, you are seeing a glimpse of things to come. The question would then be, "Do I really want to do this?" It is important for the couple to be aware of the financial commitments they are going to step into.

4. PRIMARY BELIEFS

A family's primary beliefs are fostered, nurtured, and developed in childhood. These beliefs become the foundation upon which the philosophies of the family are formulated. For instance, our family does not believe that you should finance a car before purchasing a home. We don't encourage that practice. Therefore, this has become a family practice of ours; it forms one of our primary beliefs. What are your family's beliefs built upon? Observe where the other family's theories come from. Do they base their actions on what the Bible says, or on what the world does, or on Grandma's rocking chair stories?

A person may say, "Well, you know, Grandma said..." or "Big Mama always said..." or "Papa always said..." By saying these things, the person is identifying the family's beliefs.

Discovering the foundational thoughts of every family becomes important for many reasons. For example, in child rearing, the husband and wife need to agree on the method they will use to discipline the children. Therefore, each person needs to know the other's expectations, which are usually formed based upon their

Overlooking what the other person believes will bring trouble, but carefully observing what those beliefs are will lead to harmony.

family's beliefs. Is the person making decisions based on a clinical psychologist's perspective or the immediate family's rules? Or are his or her decisions based on the Word of God? The marriage partners must understand the basis for decisions made within the union.

In discipline and in every other aspect of life in the new family nest, it is so important to know each other's beliefs. Overlooking what the other person believes will bring trouble, but carefully observing what those beliefs are will lead to harmony.

5. EMOTIONS

Before blending two families, the man and the woman need to take careful notice of how the other's family members respond to different life situations. More importantly, they need to observe how other people respond to the family members.

Let's say the person you are dating has a son named Johnny who has a habit of throwing tantrums. You notice that the whole family just ignores Johnny's tantrums. They might say, "That's just how Johnny acts. He's been like that for the past 15 years." You think that Johnny is strange, and he is. However, the whole family has tolerated his strangeness, and they expect you to tolerate it as well.

If you marry into that family without ironing out the difference of opinion as to how to respond to that strangeness, then there will be trouble in the home. If you determine that Johnny is not a good influence for your children to be around, you will end up getting into a conflict with the members of your spouse's family.

Whole people become whole only in Christ. Healed people heal people, but hurting people hurt people. Of course, you want to marry a whole, healed person, but you also need to discover the emotional status of that person's family. Emotional wholeness and health in the two families that come into the union will bring wholeness and health to the new family structure

6. FAMILY HISTORY

In order to find out about each other's family history, you are going to have to ask some questions. Each of you should ask where the other's family has lived. You should find out the family members' birthdates, and the times and places of their births. You need to know about the marriages in each other's families. How many have been successful and how many have ended in divorce?

It is important to find out about these things, because they will affect the way both of you perceive family structure. If you are dating someone whose family has been plagued with divorce, that person may think divorce is a natural escape from marital problems. Do not ignore Satan's pattern of destruction throughout that family. If the individual you are considering marrying does not have strong biblical beliefs, he or she may choose divorce as a way out when problems arise. You should pursue that relationship only if you are sure that the individual has gone to the Word of God and developed God's plan for marriage.

7. LIFE SPAN

It is important to look at the number of years marriage relationships have lasted in your potential spouse's family. You need to know how long their parents and grandparents have been married. If the grandparents have been married sixty years, the parents forty, and the uncle thirty, then your mate will have gained some insight into building a long-lasting relationship just by observing those relationships. Of course, all of those years may not have been good, but the longevity of those relationships will bring you hope.

The couple will bring two structures into their marriage, and they must create a new single structure in order to have a successful home.

On the other hand, a warning light should go on in your heart if you are at your potential spouse's family reunion and you hear something like, "There's my dad's first wife, and that's his child from his first marriage. She's divorced right now, but they have three kids. My sister never got married, but she has four kids...."

The couple must search deeper than the surface to learn about each other's family history. In order to find out whether the new family will sink or swim, the couple will have to test their abilities by going beyond the shallow water and getting into the deep water. By going into these deep levels, the dating couple will be able to determine whether their marriage will have staying power.

God has a track record in everything He has promised to do. Longevity is a key to building a successful nest. Anything that is alive, including a family, has a life span. As we just saw, a man and a woman considering marriage need to ask themselves, "How long are the marriages in that family lasting? How close do family members stay to each other? Do they keep in contact?" Answering these questions will help the couple know what will be expected of them when they blend their families and begin working toward becoming one family.

These seven components—spirituality, relationships, finances, primary beliefs, emotions, family history, and life span—will be brought into the structure of the new home when two people are joined in marriage. The couple will bring two structures into their marriage, and they must create a new single structure in order to have a successful home. We simply call that blending: to combine two entities to form something new.

Developing this new structure will be a difficult but not impossible process, especially when the two being joined are blending families from previous relationships. As we said earlier, developing a new family is work, but developing a blended family takes working overtime.

SEEK HEAVENLY INSTRUCTION

Building a strong family structure requires a willingness to take heavenly instruction—and correction, if necessary. Proverbs 12:1 NIV says, *"Whoever loves discipline loves knowledge, but he who hates correction is stupid."* If you love knowledge, then you are a wise person. If you love instruction, then you will function in wisdom. When you function in wisdom, you strengthen the structure of your home.

Let's Pray

Dear Father, in the Name of Jesus, we seek Your face today as we seek to build this new nest. We first acknowledge that we cannot do this without You, and we solicit Your help. Reveal our primary beliefs and all else that is needed to make our union successful. Help us make the necessary adjustments as we encounter obstacles, and give us the strength to endure to the end, in Jesus' Name. Amen.

Family Exercises

1. Visit with each other's families.

2. Discuss your immediate concerns.

3. Decide what your blended family's primary beliefs will be.

4. Identify patterns of destruction observed on both sides of the family, and pray about them.

5. Commit to revisiting any or all concerns as they arise.

SCRIPTURE REFERENCES

Proverbs 24:3

Matthew 7:24

Proverbs 12:1

9

NOT MINE,
NOT YOURS,
BUT OURS

9

NOT MINE, NOT YOURS, BUT OURS

As you prepare to become one family with a spouse, you must implement a number of strategic plans to assure success. Let's journey deeper into the formation of the blended family and review the variables that come into play as the family develops. All factors should be considered, and every party involved needs to be informed of the obstacles that lie ahead.

There are two major levels in a family: the primary family and the secondary family. The primary family includes the father, mother, and children. The secondary family includes grandparents, aunts, uncles, and a host

Just because you have something in the blender, it does not necessarily mean that something is blending.

of cousins and friends. For it to succeed, your family must be of utmost importance to you and all other parties involved. Remember, just because you have something in the blender, it does not necessarily mean that something is blending. As a matter of fact, if we were to put some oil and water into a blender and begin the process of blending, the two substances would appear to merge together and become one. However, unless the blender remained on indefinitely, the two entities would soon separate.

In the blended family, there are no opportunities for the parties to retreat to their corners of the boxing ring. You must stay in the middle of the ring. Remember, "Swing only when necessary, and duck when you need to!"

THE PRIMARY FAMILY

Let's examine some important factors in the formation of the primary family. In order for you to lay a strong foundation at the start of the new marriage union, one of the very first factors that must be discussed is this: You must acknowledge that this union is not ordinary—involving a single man and a single woman. Remind yourselves that this is an extraordinary union, and everyone is special in this family. You must acknowledge that this union is not God's original idea of the family, but with His help, you can make it. Then, acknowledge the important role that God must play in your union from Day One.

Once you have accepted that you are a blended family and not a copy of God's original idea, you are responsible to move on. You must trust God with every person, situation, and variable that you encounter as you enter into covenant. Through His grace and mercy, you will make it. We have discovered that blending is a continuous learning experience. It does not stop!

The very next thing to deal with is to get rid of the words *yours* and *mine* and replace them with *ours*. Acknowledge that you are in this thing together. If you are not ready to release your children to your spouse and trust that they will not be harmed, then your marriage will not work. You have a divided home, union, and marriage, and nothing permanent can be built on that kind of foundation.

You must build the new nest with the understanding that each spouse is responsible for all the children involved. Until you reach this elementary stage in the marriage, your union will always be like a roller-coaster ride—up and down. And your children will soon figure out that they have options and play a game that they will always win.

When you say "my children" and "his children," you are not taking ownership of all the children.

Note this: When you say "my children" and "his children," you are not taking ownership of all the children. The children will sense that you are not taking ownership of them as you do with the kids who came from your own loins. You must get rid of the terms *your children* and *those children*. This may seem to be a simple thing, but it is the beginning step of building a new nest and making everyone feel as if they are a part of the family.

STEVE:

During one weekend visit early in our union, the sounds of heavy coughing awakened me. Benjamin was under physical attack. He was miserable and could hardly catch his breath. I lay beside my wife, waiting for her to take the role of the mother of the house and minister to him. I expected her to leap out of bed, run down the stairs, get the cough syrup, and sit with him until he felt better. This was my vision of the kind of wife I had married. To put it mildly, it was an unrealistic and farfetched expectation.

*Needless to say, Benjamin's cough did not cease and neither did my wife's sleep. In anger, I got up and took care of "my son," a common practice of mine. Angry and disappointed, I stared into the television. My night was ruined. I thought, **Why didn't she get up? Why didn't she help "my son"?** Not long into the night, my wife* appeared out of the dark and sat beside me. Initially, I would not talk at all. Finally, with a hundred questions and accusations concerning the poor example of a mother she had been in the time of "my son's" crisis, I expressed my disappointment. Then, adding fuel to the fire that I had started, I made the point strongly that if it had been Darell coughing, she would have heard him. To my surprise, my wife turned to me and said, "You are absolutely right. I would have heard

When you remarry you are marrying more than just a man or a woman. You are uniting with a family of people.

Darell coughing. But because I did not give birth to Benjamin, Stephen, Christa, or Justin, I do not have that built-in mechanism from God working inside of me. I'm sorry, but this takes time. Please be patient with me." She then turned and went back to bed and left me pondering. This was a step toward becoming one that I had to take alone. But in time, she took ownership of all the children and their needs. There were even times when she was more sensitive to their feelings than I was, and she could pick up on their cares quicker than I could.

THE WEEKEND CHILD

As we dig deeper into the formation of the blended family, we soon discover that, as in all unions, when you remarry you are marrying more than just a man or a woman. You are uniting with a family of people. This family may include the child who is not in the home every day—who may come together with the family only on weekends. Your union involves that child as well.

THE EX-SPOUSE

The third factor that you must handle immediately in the new union is how you will deal with the ex-spouse. Agreement between husband and wife is paramount to maintain a healthy marriage. The couple must come to an agreement as to how and when each of you will communicate with the ex-spouse. Conversations with an ex-spouse should remain focused on the needs of the child or children that the two of you share. Visitations and weekend trips should be discussed within the new union and decisions conveyed to the ex-spouse. At no time should that ex-spouse be allowed to control your home! All decisions must be made internally—that is, within the new union—before being expressed to someone else.

"Healthy children are birthed out of healthy homes."

We recommend that a particular day and time be set for the child to speak to the external parent. This will keep the ex-spouse from interrupting your schedule and family time. We discovered that many times following a child's "phone visit" with the ex-spouse, the child needed some time alone to regroup and reconnect with our home. If you discover that your child is somewhat upset by the phone visit, then allow the child to communicate only by using the speakerphone, or through a conference call. In this way, you can take charge of the call if it appears to bring confusion to the heart of the innocent child.

The ultimate goals here are to remove all possibilities of confusion spreading in the mind of the child, and to keep peace within your new union. "Healthy children are birthed out of healthy homes."

THE NEEDS OF THE SECONDARY FAMILY

Thus far we have been addressing the needs of the primary family. However, some of the same rules apply to the members of the secondary family.

This secondary family includes relatives of the ex-spouse, be it the ex-wife's family or the ex-husband's family or both. Guidelines should be established with all parties, because the children did not divorce their parents, grandparents, and other relatives. Communication with the ex-grandparents will develop over time, and as the parent, you should express your expectations. Do not allow negative remarks to be made in your presence, or in your absence, concerning your new spouse. It is your

The success of the union—the glue that holds your new union together—is the Word of God, the promise of God, and the degree to which your family stays in agreement.

responsibility to handle any family matters relating to the spouse.

The rule of thumb we've used is this: I handle all of my relatives and my ex-spouse's relatives, and I clear the air of all unrealistic expectations concerning the new union. Donna handles her relatives and ex-spouse's relatives. We strongly recommend keeping the family members of both parties out of the new union until you have laid a solid foundation. Once you have established that, then you can inform everyone involved of what you expect of them.

THE QUESTION OF ADOPTION

Many blended families face the question of adoption. This is a big step to take. The level of involvement of the biological parent is a key factor in determining whether you should consider adoption in the blended family. Everyone's feelings must be taken into account, and much prayer must go forth before this monumental decision is made.

STARTING A NEW NEST

Once you have addressed these key issues, your new nest is ready for you to begin the adventure of blending two families into one. Remember, the success of the union—or rather, the glue that holds your new union together "until death do you part"—is the Word of God, the promise of God, and the degree to which your family stays in agreement.

Let's Pray

Father, we thank You for this extraordinary uniting of this family. We know that You are the God of the impossible, and we dedicate this union unto You. Do with it as You will, and continue to bless us and strengthen us each day. Our complete trust is in You, Lord. Amen!

May God bless and keep your union from this day onward.

Family Exercises

1. Discuss what the children should call both the parents and the stepparents.

2. Discuss how the family will be introduced to others.

3. Discuss how the family will handle questions from outsiders.

SCRIPTURE REFERENCES

Ephesians 5:22-28

Ephesians 6:1-4

Amos 3:3

10

LIVING FOR THE WEEKEND

10

LIVING FOR THE WEEKEND

STEVE:

I can remember the hustle and bustle of making it to the agreed location for the pick-up and the drop-off. Punctuality was a major factor in order for me to see my kids. The children always brought much excitement and anticipation as they got into the van. Everyone was greeted with hugs while Christa and Darell measured to see who was the tallest. Justin and Benjamin spent their time vying for my attention and trying to catch me up on the current professional football team statistics or the results of the most recent national basketball game. The van filled once again with the sounds of my children's voices, and my heart filled with joy. In only an hour, we would head to the airport to pick up Stephen as he came in from Oklahoma. Jonathan was at peace in my wife's *womb. We had an hour to kill as we waited for Stephen to land. Then we found out that his flight was delayed, and we lived at least forty-five minutes from the airport. Finally, the big guy arrived and we headed for home to begin our weekend. It was nearly 11:30 Friday night. I had less than forty-eight hours with them and I'd better make the best of it.*

Many blended families are structured around regular weekend visits. These usually come with a combination of anxiety, frustration, uncertainty, anticipation, and high expectations. A number of parties are affected by the blending of two families, but our emphasis will give attention to three of these: the primary parent, the secondary parent, and the stepparents.

Your agreement with your spouse and your acceptance of the children are paramount if you are to have lasting peace in your home and your union.

The primary parent is defined as the physical guardian who is responsible for taking care of the principal needs and welfare of the children. Those needs include education, general health, food, clothing, shelter, emotional stability, and so forth. The secondary parent's responsibility may be largely financial, coupled with scheduled visits filled with fun and exciting activities. This parent is trying to make up for lost time and endeavors to hide his or her guilty feelings by making every moment more memorable than the last.

The primary parent and the secondary parent are the children's biological parents, and they may or may not be married. The stepparent is the spouse of a biological parent. This is the formation of the blended family. Now join us as we take a look at the thoughts of these three parties as they participate in a typical weekend visit.

The primary parent thinks, *The bags are packed and ready to go. It's his weekend. God only knows what will go on. I really wanted to take them to that movie, but my work schedule would not permit it. I wonder if they are brushing their teeth. Is she being nice to MY children? What will they do? One thing I remember is that after the last visit they did not come back with all their clothes.*

The secondary parent thinks, *It's the weekend. I only have 48 hours to spend with my children. We must have FUN!!!*

(Note: Both the primary and secondary parent love their children, but they express that love in different ways.)

Then the stepparent may think, *It's so exhausting! Technically, they're only here for less than 48 hours. Therefore, I can tolerate it. Well...let's get ready for the fun!*

(Note: The stepparent's responsibility is to support his or her spouse and create a welcoming and emotionally stable environment for the children.) If you as the step-parent do not want the children in your home, the children and your mate will sense this, and it will breed contention in your union. Your agreement with your spouse and your acceptance of the children are paramount if you are to have lasting peace in your home and your union. Therefore, receive the children with open arms, pure motives, godly intentions, and a good attitude. Remember, the children are innocent and you need God to rectify the results of your past decisions.

The real question is, which parent are you?

48 HOURS OF FUN

Let's define the weekend visit. This visit usually consists of fun managed by the secondary family. The children enjoy these visits because they provide a way of temporary escape from the routine and structure of the primary home. The weekend visit may consist of shopping, movies, staying up late, and lots of snacks and video games. But in reality, the secondary home may lack the structure, discipline, and order of the primary home. This breeds instability in the lives of the children. The more balance there is between the routines in the two homes, the greater will be the stability of all the children involved. Those could include children who live permanently in the secondary home because they were born from the new marriage, and children who come to the home for regular weekend visits. Therefore, the need for stability is vital for all children involved.

The primary parent has the responsibility to *"train up a child in the way he should go [and in keeping with his individual gift or bent], and when he is old he will not depart from it"* (Prov. 22:6 AMP). Typically, the primary home is where the most structure and stability exist. The primary parent is responsible to provide shelter, food, and other basic needs. This parent usually is most in tune with the emotional needs of the children and meets most of their financial requirements. There is structure in that environment. In other words, the primary home is where the children find the most predictable pattern for living.

The secondary parent's home is usually very different from that of the primary parent. The responsibilities of this parent are limited—they are fewer and less demanding. This parent has the luxury of sharing only partial responsibility for the children's needs. The children experience less structure and more excitement due to the limited time they spend in the secondary parent's home. The children are away from the regimen of the primary home; therefore, they tend to favor being in the secondary home.

Our emphasis was not on how much money we spent on the children but rather on how much time we spent with them.

The "weekend parents" can make the hours pass in a number of ways. During their visit, the children are largely entertained with amusing pastimes and activities. Usually, rules and regulations are limited, allowing the children to experience more freedom than in their primary parent's home. The secondary parent's feelings of guilt could be one reason why they structure their home in this way. Because they have only a few hours to see the children, the secondary parent feels obligated to enjoy the time rather than spend it correcting them.

We have spent our visit weekends hosting family dance contests, visiting Pizza Hut, going on short vacations, and simply hanging around the house. Our emphasis was not on how much money we spent on the children but rather on how much time we spent with them. Usually these weekends took up all of our time and everything else stopped.

THE RULES CHANGE

Another thing that weekend visits consist of is altered rules for all the children. For instance, during weekend visits there is greater flexibility. The standing rules of the house, which the children are accustomed to, are usually lifted. Certain things are not required. For example, the regular bedtime schedule is lifted, the vegetables do not have to be eaten, the homework and the review of next week's spelling words are not even thought of, and there are no quiet times for reading. Baths are sometimes skipped, and the brushing of teeth is not policed.

When children are returned to the primary parent, there is usually discontent, because the children are usually out of order, undisciplined, and not clean. Book bags are missing, and the children who are returning to the primary home are unrecognizable as those who came from that home just 48 hours earlier.

The flip side of this scenario would be quite different—meaning, the children would return disciplined and well groomed, dressed in new or clean clothes, with freshly groomed hair and homework completed.

It is clear that with blended families, the structures in the homes of the biological parents are different. This creates an avenue of options for the children to abuse. This scenario can continue throughout the children's lifetimes, and it usually builds tension between the two homes and between all adults involved. Parents of children in this situation need to talk and try to agree upon the expectations for behavior in both homes. Such agreement will close the door of opportunity for the children to manipulate the adults. However, if agreement between the biological parents was possible, there might not have been a separation or divorce to begin with. Plainly said, How can two walk together unless they agree? (See Amos 3:3.)

Let's Pray

Lord Jesus, we submit our family and all of our concerns to Your guidance and direction. We trust You to tie all the loose ends together by Your power and through Your love. Father, move in the homes where our children lay their heads, and protect them from all hurt, harm, and danger. May the peace of God that surpasses all understanding keep our hearts and minds through Christ Jesus. And great shall be the peace of my children who are taught of the Lord. Amen.

Family Exercises

1. Set and maintain a schedule of weekend pick-ups for the children in order to create stability for them.

2. The stepparent and the spouse should dialogue about their feelings and expectations for visits by the children. (Honesty is necessary here.)

3. Plan activities that include academics, discipline, and fun.

4. Pray with the family at some time during the visit.

5. Host a family meeting as you and your spouse feel it is necessary.

SCRIPTURE REFERENCES

Proverbs 22:6

Amos 3:3

11

PLANNING FOR THE WEEKEND

11

PLANNING THE WEEKEND

In order to successfully become one family on the weekends, a couple needs to follow some basic guidelines. First, they must communicate well with each other. Second, they must establish clear rules for disciplining the children. Third, they must spend quality time with the children. Finally, they must create a special place in their home for each child. Now, let's look more closely at each of these guidelines.

THE NEED FOR GOOD COMMUNICATION

The first guideline for bringing a blended family together during a weekend visit involves good communication between the husband and the wife. Donna and I spent many long hours discussing the children's weekend visits. Practically all of our family's video footage was taken on the weekends when Stephen was in town. We were fortunate to have Stephen with us during his entire junior year in high school. (We will discuss those precious moments in the next chapter.) One thing we agreed upon was that when our children looked at the videos, they would see themselves and not feel left out.

Remember, your sensitivity to the needs of *each* child in your blended family is essential to the success of your family. Be careful not to overlook the feelings of the children, your spouse, or even yourself, because those feelings are crucial in building and strengthening your family.

Both you and your spouse need to communicate and decide on the rules for the weekend visits. For example, my wife and I discussed what we would do when the children arrived and what our plans would be for the weekend. On one occasion my wife recommended that we not have a "fantasy weekend" of fun, but rather spend a quiet couple of days at home with the children. We rented movies, ate popcorn, played games, talked, laughed, and then fell asleep on the sofa or the floor in each other's arms. It was wonderful!

In order to have times like these and keep the home flowing smoothly in peace and love, the husband and wife need to communicate. Communication leads to unity not only in planning activities but also in establishing rules for discipline, which is the second guideline for bringing a blended family together.

BE CLEAR ABOUT DISCIPLINE

The second guideline to follow to become one family during a weekend visit is for the couple to make sure that each child clearly understands the rules for discipline in the home. Decisions about when to discipline must be made before the children arrive. As a couple is creating a list of rules together, they need to remember that the first priority in discipline is to show the children they care about them. Proverbs 13:24 says, *"He who spares his rod hates his son, but he who loves him disciplines him promptly."* Discipline, then, comes out of the parents' love for their children as much as the desire to spend quality time with them comes from that love. Remember: *Do not stop being a parent. Raise your children, even on the weekend!*

PLAN SOME QUALITY TIME WITH THE CHILDREN

The third guideline to having a successful weekend blend is to plan quality time with the children. This means that you must identify with their interests and desires. It means that you must spend time listening to your children and sharing your vision for your family. This is important because it creates a time when the children can get to know you and your spouse. Love usually grows when you spend time with someone and when you show you care. You can't put a price on quality time, but it demands that you be fully "there."

As you bring your blended family together, plan to do homework with the children. Talk to them about what they're doing at school, and be a part of their education. Then end your weekends on a high note by attending church and worshiping God together.

We have spent many of our family weekends celebrating each of the children's accomplishments. We all traveled down to Oklahoma to watch and video Stephen's state-championship football game. We all watched Justin, Darell, and Benjamin as they played for a local Kansas City community football team, the Wolverines. Our great Lady Pirate, Christa, played in several girls' basketball games for Platte County High School. Jonathan's activities have ranged from T-ball to flag football to basketball to singing in a junior ensemble, and we made it to them all. Our children have been active throughout their middle school and high school years both at school and in the church. Occasionally, my wife and I have been forced to divide our time. While one attended a choir concert and tae kwon do, the other went to piano lessons and football games. From Omaha to St. Louis to Jackson, Mississippi, to Fort Jackson, and Georgia, our children have taken us all over the place. We are pleased to announce that Stephen, Justin,

By following these four guidelines, parents will help the children feel at home, even if they are only with the family on the weekends.

Benjamin, and Darell have all finished high school and joined the Army. Christa has graduated from high school, and Penni has received a double master's degree. Jonathan is currently in middle school, and he will be with us for a little while longer.

Notice that spending quality time with a child does not cost a lot. However, it makes a bigger impact on a child's heart than any expensive gift. The important thing is to show that you care.

CREATE A SPECIAL PLACE FOR EACH CHILD

Another guideline for becoming one family during weekend visits is to create a special place in your home for each child. This shows that you are planning your life and including them in it. Having a place to call their own while they are with you is important to them.

For example, everyone had a special shelf for each child to have their toys. Each child had their own bed and sleeping bag. When movie time came, everyone had their own sleeping bag and spot on the floor. We had our blankets, the children had their sleeping bags, and we would all watch movies together.

As the dynamics and structure of your home change, you will need to revisit these guidelines. For example, the arrival of a child born to your union could cause the guidelines to change. Continued consideration for your family must be a primary goal while you are becoming one. By following these four guidelines, parents will help the children feel at home, even if they are only with the family on the weekends. Parents will also be setting precedents for the family structure if and when weekend visits by a child become permanent living arrangements. We will take up that issue in the next chapter.

Let's Pray

Father, in the Name of Jesus, we commit our family to You. We trust You to perfect those things that concern us. Move by Your Spirit in our lives as we plan these special times with our children. May these times be peaceful, fulfilling, and memorable for each of us, and may we grow in Your strength each day as we are apart from each other. Keep our children in the spirit of peace, and guard their hearts from any thoughts or imaginations that are contrary to Your Word and Your plan and purpose for their lives. Amen!

Family Exercises

1. Review the guidelines explained in this chapter and discuss how they can apply to your home.

2. Plan your weekends together and consider all parties involved.

3. Always create an atmosphere in which you and your spouse can be honest about your feelings. Check with each other regularly.

SCRIPTURE REFERENCES

Proverbs 13:24

Psalm 9:10

Psalm 119:165

12

WHEN THE WEEKEND VISIT BECOMES PERMANENT

12

WHEN THE WEEKEND VISIT BECOMES PERMANENT

Many times, blended families find themselves unexpectedly preparing to receive one or more of the "weekend visit" children permanently into their homes. Parents of blended families should keep the attitude that at any given time your home might become the permanent residence for any of the children who have not been living with you. Each child must feel welcome. Keep in mind that when weekend visits become permanent, you must adjust the structure of the secondary home for it to become the primary home for those children.

STEVE:

Waking from a deep sleep, I hear the phone ring. As I fumble for the handset, my wife answers quickly, and then hands it to me. It's our oldest son, Stephen. "Dad, can I come live with you?" he asks. Remembering that my wife and I had already discussed that a day like this might come, we had already decided that we would readily receive all of the children into our home if they cried out for help. Well, here we were, and the first to call was Stephen. Our answer was, "Sure!" and the preparations began.

How prepared are you to hear, "Can I come live with you?" Take time to make the necessary plans before you find yourself in this situation. Understand that when you say yes, there will be significant changes, again, in the family dynamics—spiritually, socially, and financially. Even knowing all of these things, we were not totally prepared. But without hesitation, we immediately said yes.

One of the greatest problems of a blended family will arise when the children discover the power of their options.

FIX ANOTHER PLATE

There's really no way to predict when weekend visits will become permanent. In some cases, the courts may order that the children be placed with the other parent. That can give the family receiving the child some time to prepare for the structural change. But there are also times when a crisis in the home brings about a need for emergency occupancy. When you face such times, the only thing we can say to you is, "Fix another plate!"

In our case, the change happened overnight. There was no time to think or react—only to do. It was really just that simple. In one night, we went from having two children in the home to having all five boys living with us. We changed instantly from a family of four for dinner to a family of seven. And by the time Penni graduated, married, divorced, and returned to our home, we were a family of ten.

DONNA:

"Pack your bags. I'll make the arrangements to bring you home," my husband said. There was no need to react or panic because we had already discussed this possibility early in our marriage and decided to receive the children.

DISCOVERING THE OPTIONS

One of the greatest problems of a blended family will arise when the children discover the power of their options. This usually occurs when they begin to choose which home provides

Remain the adult, remain the parent, and keep your control.

the most entertainment and the least amount of structure and opposition. Be careful here. If your home becomes their top choice, it does not necessarily indicate that they love you more and the other parent less. Know that their vote is cast based on the environment that provides the least resistance. You have been awarded the privilege of having sleepless nights and restless days, making emergency stops at your house, and dealing with the urge to take a drive on your lunch break to check on your children. Your cell phone minutes will soon disappear, and you will find that you have long-distance calls to pay for that you did not make. When the children nominate you for "home of the year," be alert and look closely at what is really going on. Finally, do not give in to thoughts that suggest that you have won the battle with your ex-spouse, because there are no winners in a divorce.

Deal With the Guilt

Stand your ground. Do not fall prey to the games of your children and do not buy in to their manipulations. Remain the adult, remain the parent, and keep your control. Feelings of guilt will try to overtake you and keep you from making sound decisions concerning the best place for the children to reside. Do not be afraid to obey God, when it is in the best interest of your children to do so, and never allow yourself to feel guilty in the process. Acknowledge the guilt but do not feed it.

SUCCESSFUL BLENDING

When the weekend visits become permanent, the family will need to take several steps to make a smooth transition toward becoming one. Here are some guidelines for the new family to follow to create a successful blend.

- Parents: communicate your expectations to one another.

- Plan the house rules.

- Clearly describe your expectations to the children.

- Establish a time for the secondary parent to call.

Following these suggestions is necessary in order to give each child time to adjust to the change of an enlarged family. Now let's look at each of these guidelines more closely to see how we can create a new, successful, permanent family structure.

COMMUNICATE EXPECTATIONS TO YOUR SPOUSE

When weekend visits become permanent, the first guideline for a smooth transition into full time blending is for each spouse to communicate their expectations to one another.

Identifying and communicating expectations is the first step toward a pleasant transition from visits to permanently becoming one family.

DONNA:

When Steve's children came to live in our house, I asked him, "Baby, what do you expect from me as it pertains to our children?" I was part of this blended family, and my husband's expectations were very important to me. Clarifying what you and your spouse expect will resolve a great deal of conflict as you grow in your union. After I asked the question, Steve turned it around and asked, "What do you expect from me?"

I told him that I expected the children to respect me both in my presence and in my home. I made no demand on any of the children to love me, because love is developed over time. I also expected the son that I brought into the union to respect my husband as the head of the house. Identifying and communicating expectations is the first step toward a pleasant transition from visits to permanently becoming one family.

PLAN THE HOUSE RULES

Once the couple clearly understands one another's expectations, they need to take the second step toward bringing their blended family together. That step is planning the rules of the house. Both spouses need to be involved in deciding what the rules will be, and what the children can and cannot do. After they accomplish that, they will be ready for the third step.

DISCUSS EXPECTATIONS AND RULES
WITH THE CHILDREN

The third step in becoming one family when one or more children are added permanently is to call a family meeting with the children and clearly communicate to them your expectations and rules. After you present the rules, question each child—one at a time—to make sure everyone heard and understood them. Take time to answer any questions that may arise. Be prepared for the meeting to take some time. The longer the list of rules, the longer the meeting will be.

SET A TIME FOR THE SECONDARY PARENT TO CALL

In order to transition peacefully from weekend visits to a permanent blend, you must set a time for the children's other parent to call them. The other parent is not a part of your family structure and doesn't live according to your house rules. Therefore, you need to establish a time when you are able to monitor the calls until the children and the other parent are able to conduct a call without you.

For example, you might tell the other parent that he or she can call Sundays between 6 and 8 P.M. If that's not a good time, don't let the other parent call the school or Grandma's house to speak to the children. That would mean someone else is establishing a new structure for them. Don't allow the other parent to undermine your new family structure, because that will lead to confusion not only in the children, but between you and your spouse. It will bring division into your home. The Word of God says, *"If a house is divided against itself, that house cannot stand"* (Mark 3:25 NIV). So set aside a time for the other parent to be involved in the kids' lives through scheduled phone conversations.

GIVE THE CHILDREN A REALISTIC ADJUSTMENT PERIOD

Allow the children just coming into your home a realistic amount of time to adjust. They have to adjust to the new setting, the new stepparent, the new structure, the new rules, and so forth. The children have a lot on their minds. For example, they may wish that the structure they see in the new home had existed in their original home so that there never would have been a divorce in the first place. They may be trying to reconcile the desire to hold on to the past with a desire to make things smooth in the new family structure.

It is also important to allow the children to hold on to their memories of the time when their biological parents were together. Allow them to harbor the memories of joy in their hearts. This will aid in the health and stability of their emotions.

Let's Pray

Dear Father, we thank You for our family and that Your hand is upon us to do Your will. Lord, as we make this change to a more permanent structure, lead and guide us. We thank You in advance that each of the children will adjust to the new family structure and that we, the spouses and parents, will remain in agreement. May Your blessings be upon us now, in Jesus' Name. Amen.

Family Exercises

1. Plan your house rules and stick to them. (Make revisions only when absolutely necessary.)

2. Have a family meeting to communicate expectations and to go over the rules.

3. Schedule and plan special time with each child regularly.

SCRIPTURE REFERENCES

Mark 3:25

Philippians 1:6

Philippians 3:14

13

WE CANNOT

CHANGE THE PAST

13

WE CANNOT
CHANGE THE PAST

DONNA:

I know what it feels like to be a child in a divorce situation. My father and mother divorced when my sister and I were girls, and my mother raised us. I have a picture of my father, my mother, my sister, and me. This was my family structure when I was born. The picture was taken December 19, 1985, the day of my graduation, the day I received my master's degree from Louisiana State University. I had never had a picture before of just the four of us. Even today, I desire to have that family I grew up in to be whole. This is the picture of my family that I had in my mind, and that day I was afforded the family structure I'd always wanted. That picture sits on my kitchen counter today.

Make efforts to create new memories, while holding on to the old.

My mom and my sister have died and are no longer here. My father is alive and remarried. I also have three older sisters and two brothers who were born through my father's first marriage. I was privileged to see them sometimes twice a year. Our visits were always pleasant, and I truly enjoyed being the little sister. I am thankful today for my mother's determination to make everyone feel at home in our house.

Parents, allow your children to hold on to their memories. Allow them to talk about those memories, because when you do, you are allowing them to heal. No one has the power to change the past. Therefore, every time you attempt to stop the children and their parents from holding on to the memories, you delay the healing process. Allow them to talk about them and ask questions.

Be careful not to try to erase your children's past by creating a new future. Make efforts to create new memories, while holding on to the old. One way we have tried to do this is by starting a keep box. In the box we have pictures, holiday cards, and memoirs of the years our family has been together. Donna has created scrapbooks for each of the children, and each book holds the same pictures of all of our family outings. Steve has purposed to save pictures, trophies, newspaper clipping, and sports paraphernalia from each of the children's athletic activities.

Each child in a blended family is key to the success of that blended family.

The memories you create will become a part of everyone's repertoire, and each will become a point of contact for many family gatherings to come. The annual "Houpe Family Dance Contests" by the pool have brought tremendous times of laughter and jokes to many family gatherings. At times, all the kids have been at home and there were no new movies at the video rental store, so we decided to look at some old family videos. The children might have been everywhere in the house, but in just minutes, everyone gathers around the television, and we relive the moments all over again. There is no greater joy than when a family can relive happy moments together.

EVERYONE SAYS "I DO"

When two people decide to say "I do" to each other, they may think they have conquered the world. But each child in a blended family is key to the success of that blended family. All of the children have to say "I do." Saying "I do" doesn't mean that the children no longer love their mom or their dad. Rather, saying "I do" means that they have found room in their hearts to receive

Children, if a parent is guiding you according to the Word of God, he or she will not direct you wrong.

another person's love. Understand that this may not happen overnight, but if the family serves God and walks in His love, the time of saying "I do" to this situation will eventually come for all.

THE POWER OF AGREEMENT

Before this new blended family can become one and walk in the vision God has for it, everyone needs to walk in agreement. Before this family can stand before God and receive all of the blessings that He has in store for them, each one in the family needs to say "I do." Parents, give the children time to adjust to the new structure so that the family can walk in agreement. During this adjusting period, the children also need to remember what God says about discipline. For example, Proverbs 12:1 NIV says, *"Whoever loves discipline loves knowledge, but he who hates correction is stupid."* And Proverbs 13:1 says, *"A wise son heeds his father's instruction, but a scoffer does not listen to rebuke."*

We could summarize the message of these two verses by saying this: "A wise child will take heed to his parents' instruction (and that includes the instruction of the stepfather or stepmother when it's based on God's Word), but a foolish child doesn't listen to rebuke or correction."

Children, if a parent is guiding you according to the Word of God, he or she will not direct you wrong. When the parent says no and you don't understand it, you need to know it's only to protect you. Stop fighting your parents, for they are praying for you and looking out for your well-being.

Parents, God tells you in Proverbs 19:18, *"Chasten your son while there is hope, And do not set your heart on his destruction."* Correct your children while there is hope. When children are about twelve years old, they begin to choose their paths. Most educators agree that the middle school grades are the most difficult in which to teach children. At about this time in life, children begin searching for their own identity.

Chastening, then, has to come before this time. The most intense training should happen while there is hope during those first twelve years— the habit-forming years. Habits formed during those years will create the children's character, and their character will dictate their choices.

These times will solidify your relationship with each child and lead toward unity in the whole family structure.

The child who is wise will listen and follow the parents' instruction, but the child who will not listen and follow is stupid. That's from the Word of God.

SPEND SPECIAL TIME WITH EACH CHILD

DONNA:

The first Saturday of every month, I like to set aside special one-on-one time with each of my boys. While with each one, we discuss what's going on in his life. I might say, "What happened this week? What's been the hardest thing about playing football? What's been the hardest thing through those exams? What do you least like about school? Tell me about this girl you like."

I can only tell you that these few minutes alone with each son have brought us closer together. This time is intimate and personal. Trust is established and secrets are shared. But on top of it all, the greatest benefit is that when we are finished, I have sons whom I do not recognize because their faces, ears, and noses are clean, and their hair has been washed. Hallelujah!

Whatever you decide to do during your time together, create and maintain quality time with each of your children individually. You could take your son out to dinner. You could make a candlelight dinner at home just for you and your daughter and dress up for it. What you do doesn't need to be costly. It's the quality of the time spent with each child that matters. These times will solidify your relationship with each child and lead toward unity in the whole family structure.

In fact, that is what blending is: starting over again and again to make certain that the family and every member in it is healthy and strong. When we learn to follow God's Word in every part of our family structure, we will find peace and wholeness in our hearts and in our homes. We will discover, as recorded in Psalm 133:1, how good and pleasant it is to live in unity.

Let's Pray

HELP, LORD! You know the thoughts and plans that You have for us, thoughts and plans for our welfare and peace and not for evil, to give us hope in our final outcome for our blended family. Show us Your plan that we may make it plain for our children as we become one unit, in Jesus' Name. Amen.

Family Exercises

1. Husband and wife—sit down together and discuss these questions:

    a. What is easiest when all the children are gone?

    b. What is hardest when all the children are gone?

    c. What do you least like when all the children are with you?

2. Make daily confessions from the Word of God to strengthen your family.

3.   Start *your* family's traditions.

4.   Create *your* annual family function.

5.   Decide on the way or ways you want to capture your family's happy times. Be diligent and stick with it.

SCRIPTURE REFERENCES

Amos 3:3

Proverbs 12:1

Proverbs 13:1

Proverbs 19:18

Psalm 133:1

14

LET GOD LEAD

14

LET GOD LEAD

As the blended family becomes one, we need to learn to let God lead. Have you ever listened to an orchestra at the beginning of a performance? You hear a great racket. There is no harmony among the instruments. The sounds of discord and confusion fill the room. It sounds almost as if the members of the orchestra are untrained or novices. But when the conductor steps up to the podium and raises his baton, everyone comes to attention and prepares to begin. Even the percussionist holding the cymbals—whose part may require him to play only once near the very end of the piece—stands ready for the performance. The maestro has the attention of every performer, whether he has a major role or a minor one. The stage is set. The audience, nearly holding its breath, awaits the first notes. As each member of the orchestra follow the maestro's lead, a heavenly sound fills the room. The audience embraces the majestic music of the symphony, and the musicians are equally pleased to be performing together.

In our blended family, Jesus is the maestro. With all of the challenges parents face in rearing a blending family, we must play our part as the maestro leads. This will be difficult, if we are not clear on when we are to play it. And when others are not clear on the parts they are to play, confusion arises. But Jesus, the maestro, can take an impossible situation and make beautiful blending harmonies out of it.

If you understood that illustration, then you are beginning to grasp the dynamics of the blended family. The husband and the wife play the major parts. If they do not get their parts right, then the children will not get theirs right either. As the parents read their parts and follow the maestro's lead, the children will be able to do the same.

All parents— whether biological or stepparent— must have the authority to be a parent to all of the children.

Therefore the parents must agree on the part that each of them must play in the blended family. Speaking plainly, we are talking about job descriptions. To explain this, the biological parents must concentrate on those things that must be done to promote the best interests of all of the children. The biological parents must put their differences aside and be the adults. All bitterness, anger, and strife must end and the needs and well-being of the children must take priority. The stepparent must also be clear about his or her part in this scenario, but that part is not the major one during the initial stages of bringing a blended family together. However, the time will come when the stepparent's part must be defined and made clear to everyone involved. Lastly, the children's part demands that they respect all the people in authority around them. Those people are helping the children fulfill their purpose.

Simply put, all parents—whether biological or stepparent—must have the authority to be a parent to all of the children. Parenting is the art of rearing children. Thus, each adult must have the liberty to give sound advice to the children involved in the family and make solid decisions for their benefit. Otherwise, complications will arise when discipline is needed. If the hands of the stepparent are tied when it comes to reprimanding the children, then authority has been shifted to the children. You will know this has happened when you hear, "You can't do that! You are not my momma," or "You are not my daddy!" In a blended family where this is the case, the biological parents, a bitter ex-spouse, or the extended family have stripped the stepparent of authority.

My wife and I have allowed members of our extended family to assist us with our children only if they agree to keep the standards we have set. We have had to remove enough debris of hurts and pains from our children.

They don't need any more piled on them. Therefore, we are very selective about who keeps them and who we allow to speak into their lives. Our family would not succeed if the children thought that they did not have to listen to my wife or me.

DONNA:

I remember being seven months pregnant with Jonathan, and we had the kids for the weekend. It was a Friday night and my husband had gone to dinner with a pastor friend of his. I was downstairs watching the television, probably a Lifetime movie, and the children were upstairs playing. Steve was not gone long before it felt as if the ceiling was going to cave in as the children wrestled in their bedrooms. The noise filled the house and was so loud that I could not hear what was being said on the television. I marched up the stairs six times only to threaten that I would tell their father if the noise did not cease. I suppose I did that because we had the children only for the weekend. I was trying to avoid being nominated as "Mean Stepmother of the Year" and never told on them, but I was losing my house.

On my seventh trip up the stairs, I knew that I had to do something or I would eventually grow bitter and hate the children's weekend visits. When my husband arrived home sometime after midnight, he asked for the usual report: "How were the kids?" I knew it was time to tell. I began my story with the oldest and continued to the youngest, strongly expressing my frustration. The early morning silence was broken by the sounds of screams, yells, kicks, and leaps. I stepped into my role in the family. There are times as a stepparent we can hold things back too long and not tell it all. The children from that point on realized that I would tell Dad, and I never had that problem with the children again.

Right now maybe your family is not exhibiting the harmony and beauty of an in-tune orchestra. You might be questioning whether remarriage can really overcome the chaotic aftermath of a divorce. You might even be wondering if the difficulties you are experiencing in your new marriage and blending family are punishment for past mistakes. Our advice to you is, hang in there. If you have sought God's will about your remarriage and your blended family, and you are doing what He has told you to do, then let your peace come from knowing that you are in His will.

Once you have established God's vision for your family, share it with your children. By doing this, you will all know where you are going, and it will be easier for Jesus, the maestro, to conduct the orchestra of your family as it becomes one.

To sum up, then, there will be harmony in the blended family when the husband and wife clearly define their roles based upon the Word of God. Once you have established God's vision for your family, share it with your children. By doing this, you will all know where you are going, and it will be easier for Jesus, the maestro, to conduct the orchestra of your family as it becomes one. You will no longer sound like individual instruments, each playing its own tune. Instead, you will be working together under the guidance of the Master to create a beautiful symphony.

We all need change, and the way to start change is through prayer. We are not only physical beings, but spiritual beings as well. We have the God-given authority to go into the unseen realm through prayer and bring about change. Please join us in this final prayer.

Let's Pray

In Jesus' Name, we render helpless and powerless every spirit that is trying to destroy our family and keep us from the will of God. And in the Name of Jesus, we declare that our family will stay together. Amen.

SCRIPTURE REFERENCES

Proverbs 19:18

Ephesians 6:1–4

Ephesians 5:22–33

FROM THE CHILDREN

FROM THE CHILDREN
STEPHEN (AGE 25)

Question. What are the things that come to your mind as you think about the first time you were introduced to Justin, Benjamin, Christa, and Darell?

Stephen. One of the first things I think about is Darell. I always wanted brothers and sisters. I didn't have any living with my Mom in Oklahoma. Darell was the first one of my brothers and sisters that I met. I think about the first Christmas I came down and Dad told me he was married. It was weird because I had just visited during the summer and he was single, and Whoa! I came back at Christmas and he was married.

Q. You said it was weird, but was it uncomfortable for you?

S. It wasn't uncomfortable. I wasn't uncomfortable with Darell or Mrs. Donna, as I used to call her. I was more uncomfortable with being around Dad, because I hadn't been around Dad that much at that point in time.

Q. You met Justin, Benjamin, and Christa a few days later. What were your thoughts then?

S. They were happy thoughts, but at the same time there was a downside to it because they always had to leave. There were fun times, but it was kind of difficult because Dad was going through a transition. It was a big transition for Darell and Mom also. But I think it was especially difficult for Dad because he was trying to make everyone happy. I had an easier time building a relationship with Darell before any of my biological siblings because they were going through so many changes.

Q. There was a time during your junior year in high school that you asked to stay with your dad. What brought that about?

One of the positive things that pretty much sums up everything in my experience being raised in this family is, it can be done with the help of God.

S. I wanted to be with my dad because I hadn't had an opportunity to be with him. I also missed the youth church at Harvest Church (in Kansas City, Mo., founded and pastored by Steve Houpe) because it really made an impact on my life. The times I was able to come up and visit opened my eyes to see that the kinds of things I was experiencing at home, in my neighborhood, weren't happening everywhere. I really wanted a change of environment. The one year I spent in Kansas City had a great impact on my life. I didn't even know God before I moved to Kansas

City. Everything wasn't always peaches and cream, but it was a positive year for me.

Q. You went into the military at your dad's request and have been discharged. Where are you now?

S. I'm 25 years old. Life has brought a lot of changes. I'm married with three children—a son my wife had when I married her, a daughter I fathered while in the Army, and a daughter by my wife.

Q. What is one thing you experienced growing up in a blended family that you would like to avoid in your blended family?

S. One of the things that I saw growing up was my father getting frustrated with Darell or Mrs. Donna because he didn't understand why they did some things. Not that what they did was wrong, but it was different from the way he, I, Justin, or Ben would do things. Sometimes I find myself getting frustrated with my son because he doesn't do everything like I do, because he's not from me. I never wanted to do that. But I've learned that everyone is different, and just because they do things differently, it's not wrong. That also has been a challenge for me with my wife, because we are from totally different backgrounds.

Q. What are one or two positive things you learned growing up in a blended family that you would like to implement in your family?

S. One of the positive things that pretty much sums up everything in my experience being raised in this family is, it can be done with the help of God.

From the Children
Justin (Age 21)

Question. Think back to when you were nine or ten years old and your parents were separating. How did that make you feel?

Justin. I really didn't understand what was going on. Mostly what I felt was anger.

Q. Why were you angry?

J. It was how I responded to things.

Q. Where did this anger come from?

J. When I was little, I was always mad.

Q. What were ways you expressed your anger?

J. I expressed my anger by tearing up stuff and fighting with Ben all the time.

Q. Within a year your family was making a new transition—you, Ben, and Christa were living in a new house, and Dad was living alone. Then you discovered that you had an older brother, Stephen; and your Dad had a new wife; and you now had a new little brother, Darell. First tell us, how did you feel when you discovered that you had a big brother?

J. I had mixed feelings. I had always wanted a big brother, but it was weird being knocked off the top. It was confusing. I wanted a big brother and I had him, but you're not able to function when things start shifting around and new things happen. Things changed and it was a drastic change. You were doing one thing one day, and the next day you were told, "This is your big brother." Then you have the hurt of not knowing that you had a big brother and you've been wanting a big brother all of your life. There was hurt from feeling...I won't say betrayed, but lied to. Because even if you don't tell something, it's just as much lying as telling a lie.

Q. Now you have a stepbrother and a new little brother running around. How did you feel about that?

If you know that you are about to blend, you can sit down and prepare for it. You don't take a test without preparing for it.

J. That was even harder to get used to—someone being in our house, especially when we wanted to be there after the divorce and couldn't be. One day we came home and there was someone there. It's hard when you're little because you're thinking, *"Who is this in my room playing with my toys?"* And me being the oldest and controlling everything, it was hard to get used to or respond to. I was upset. At first, I thought, *"Who are these people?"* Everything has always been forced on us. Things are one way and then it changes. We have had no say in what has transpired, or known before it happened, or even been a part of it. I feel like everything just happened and you have to deal with it.

Q. How do you help a family that knows they are about to blend not to force things upon the children?

J. If you know that you are about to blend, you can sit down and prepare for it. You don't take a test without preparing for it. If you sit down and explain the situation in a way that the children can understand instead of throwing them into the situation, they won't be bumping heads.

Q. Then adding icing to the cake, Jonathan was born. Was Jonathan easier to deal with than Darell and Stephen?

J. Jonathan was easy. We would still bump heads, but by then Darell was accepted. It was the excitement of having a new baby brother. We could all celebrate that because he is the connecter and he has a little bit of everybody. He's the one who brings us all together.

Q. What's the greatest time you've had as a family?

J. The times when we were out by the pool having a barbecue and having the dance contest.

From the Children
Benjamin (Age 20)

Question. What was the hardest part of blending the family for you?

Benjamin. The hardest part was sharing our "Dad" with a little boy and a new wife. At one moment we were a family and not long after that, he was in our home, playing with our toys, in our bed, and calling our father "Dad."

Q. How did you adjust with a new stepmother?

B. Adjusting to the new mother was hard at first. I was battling with the fact that my stepmother was doing all the things that real moms do, like helping with my homework, buying school clothes, cooking, shopping for us, etc. and yet, I still struggled. Finally, after a while, I realized two things: she made my day happy; and if God set this up, I had to accept it with no grudges.

Love those who love you. And if you feel that they truly love you, then extend the love back.

Q. What would you say to a child in a blended family?

B. Love those who love you. And if you feel that they truly love you, then extend the love back.

FROM THE CHILDREN
DARELL (AGE 18)

Question. What are some of the things that come to your mind as you have just watched a video of your first year together as a family?

Darell. The way everyone has grown—their different personalities and ways. Everyone has grown and matured so much.

Q. What are two things that you remember that were the best times for you or the most difficult times?

D. The most difficult times were when we were little and all scattered apart. You don't understand why everyone is over here and over there. The best times were when we were all together. We didn't have to have any gifts. We would just sit there laughing, talking, playing, and having fun.

Divorce is something that everybody in the family goes through—it's not just the parents.

Q. What is one thing you have learned from your household that you will take into your family?

D. Divorce is something that everybody in the family goes through—it's not just the parents. It's something I wouldn't want to go through. I want to find the right one with my first choice.

FROM THE CHILDREN
CHRISTA (AGE 17)

Question. We just saw a clip from your family at your Dad's 42nd birthday. You were living with your mom and visiting on the weekends. When you think about those times, what comes to your mind now?

Christa. I want to make sure when I grow up that my kids don't have to experience that—having to go back and forth, one week with Mom and one week with Dad. You get to see your brothers this week; you don't get to see your brothers another week because you're at another house. Having to readjust from one house to the next, catching back up with my brothers, living one way in one house and one way in another— just when I get settled in it's time to leave again. Not being able to be the same consistently is kind of confusing.

No matter whom you encounter in your life, no matter who turns their back on you, or who supports you— you will always have a family.

Q. What was the hardest part of it all when you think about being six years old at that time?

C. Going back and forth. Being so young, in my mind, I wanted to be in both places. But I knew it couldn't be that way. I had to face the facts as they were. I'll see my Mom when I'm with her; and I'll see Mom, Dad, and all my brothers when I'm with them.

Q. How did you feel when you first met Stephen?

C. I don't exactly remember my first time actually meeting Stephen. But I remember asking why I didn't know about him. This was directed toward my mother. I asked her that.

Q. Tell us about one of the most memorable times you will cherish as a girl growing up with five brothers.

C. We were all here and we were swimming. We had the dance contest and Stephen got up to dance. We had other parties when everybody was there except Stephen. But this was one particular time when we were all together. All the kids were together.

Q. What are two principles you will take to your family?

C. No matter whom you encounter in your life, no matter who turns their back on you, or who supports you—you will always have a family. No matter what family does to you, they will always be your family. Another thing I've learned is, love who loves you.

FROM THE CHILDREN
JONATHAN (AGE 10)

Jonathan was birthed into a blended family. He discovered that he had four brothers and a sister, but we did not have a typical family. He began to ask questions as to who Darell's father and Christa's mother were. His understanding of the family was not so clear.

Question. What are some of the things that were confusing to you about your family structure?

Jonathan. Darell started talking about wanting to go to his dad and I said, "Huh?" I didn't know who he was talking about. I thought he was talking about our dad, not somebody else.

Q. How did you walk through that?

J. I asked questions.

You're still part of the family no matter what.

Q. What is one thing that you remember from the family that was difficult for you?

J. When Ben, Justin, and Christa would go somewhere and Darrell would go somewhere and I didn't go.

Q. How did that make you feel?

J. Sad and left out of the picture, like I wasn't part of the family.

Q. What were some of the good times you remember?

J. When everybody was together and we just sat back and had fun. That was at Thanksgiving.

Q. What is one time in particular that was special and you'll never forget?

J. When we went to California right before Justin went into the Army.

Q. What would you like to say to a little boy or girl like yourself who is in a blended family and their brothers and sisters don't have the same Mom and Dad as them?

J. Don't feel left out. You're still part of the family. Just play along with it. You're still part of the family no matter what.

FROM THE CHILDREN
PENNI (AGE 27)

Question. What was your first encounter dealing with your blended family?

Penni. My first encounter was on one of my summer holiday visits. I think we were going to a church picnic, and I remember Darell's clothes weren't ironed. It was a reality check that it wasn't just myself, Darell, and Mrs. Houpe. It was my auntie, Darell, and a whole bunch of other kids. The priorities that we had before were different now. It wasn't just what are we needing. We were literally taking two families and blending them together, and things were different.

Q. What were two things or experiences that were difficult for you?

P. One difficult aspect of everything initially was when my auntie was married. It was the first time I realized that I was a niece and not a daughter. Because I was younger, I didn't understand why I was left in Louisiana. Of course, now knowing the spiritual side of things, I know that a lot of mind games were being played—that you're just the niece and not the daughter, and they don't have to take you to Kansas City. And for the first time, I was forced to live with a mother who never mothered me. I was dealing with all of those struggles.

My auntie was leaving Louisiana and I wasn't going. The reason I had to stay was because I was getting ready to graduate from high school at the top of my class. I didn't want to lose my scholarships. The reasons for staying sounded good, but when you're left, it seems totally different. You think, *"We could have worked around this or something. Was it that deep? I can go to junior college."* I didn't care. I knew I just wanted to go. But the choice was to leave me in Louisiana.

So, there was bitterness and anger. I thought, *"I don't care. It's clear that you don't love me as much as you say you love me."* I didn't want to hear the God side and God told me...I didn't want to hear any of that. I was left!

That left me in a state and a position I had never been in before. I take that back. I had been there before, when my grandmother died. That was another person who left me. It was almost the same thing all over again. Somebody was leaving again. I had gotten to a point where I said, "Okay, people are leaving; I don't care anymore." So, defensiveness, bitterness, and anger were there for a while. But as I visited and came to see everyone in Kansas City, I had to make quite an adjustment. It wasn't just blending with the family but blending into a different culture, blending in a new city—just blending as a whole.

Because I was a senior in high school and I still had to go through college, I became the summertime-holiday child. I came some holidays and some summers. Keep in mind I was still forced to live with my mother and bond with my mom. So, I couldn't go all of the time. And whatever feelings I did have about Kansas City or about my auntie, they had to almost completely leave me when I left Kansas City. I had to go back to my mom, who also in her own way was bitter that my auntie had left. I had to contain all the issues, feelings, pains, the happiness, the sadness; everything had to be contained once I went back to Louisiana.

Another difficult experience for me was my uncle. I remember when my uncle first came down to Louisiana and met my boyfriend for the first time. The first thing he said was, "That's not it." I was thinking, *What do you know about it? You don't even know him.* I didn't realize the role that a father plays in a girl's life. I didn't understand and know what all a father has to bring to a daughter's life. I didn't understand how my uncle could say, "He's not the one," and he didn't even know him. That was very difficult for me. That was the first time he acted in a role as a father figure (as a whole). When I was growing up with my auntie, my mother, and my grand-mother, I never had a father figure to correct me, congratulate me, applaud me, affirm me, or do all those things a father is supposed to do, even though my mother was married the bulk of my life. He was my mother's husband, not my stepfather. In getting older, I realized that there is a difference. There can be a father in the home, but he may not have an active role. I think that was the first time in my whole life that a male actually said no to me. I thought, *"How could you say no to me, when you don't even know me like that?"* That was my first major encounter not only with a blended family, but with the role of a father in my life.

Q. Were you excited when you decided to move to Kansas City permanently?

P. I was very excited for a number of reasons. But leading up to my moving here, prior to my graduating from college, my mom died. Of course there was pain, and I went through the mourning process. But I knew instantly when I walked across the stage on May 12th for my graduation where I was going. And it was confirmed by my auntie that I was welcome. And it was reaffirmed by my uncle that I was going to come to Kansas City to help serve in the ministry. So, I came with a heart and understanding that I was here to help. I came into the blended family as an adult. So, that was a little different. I went from living by myself, paying my own bills, going to school, doing what I had to do to make it, and having all the liberties and freedoms in the world...now I'm 22 and living at home with my parents. So, I had to make some adjustments.

Q. You were living with a blended family full-time. What was that like?

P. Oh, wow! It was a test. It was a test of every part of my body, my senses, and everything. Each one of the children had different personalities. Each one of them, I believe, had different motives, not in a bad way. Each one of them loved and accepted me differently at different times and in different ways and liked me for different reasons.

Because I knew that, it was kind of hard. Coming in as an adult, I couldn't come in playing. There was a level of respect that I had to gain. I was not a child anymore. When I used to come and visit as a kid, I was 17, 18, and 19 years old. Now, I was coming back as an adult. When Mom and Dad were gone, everyone had to listen to me. I had the authorization to discipline them. They went from "Hey P!" to "Yes, ma'am" and "No, ma'am." That was the hardest thing—to gain their respect. And in time, I gained all of their respect. The main thing is that they saw me helping. I wasn't a moocher. I didn't come in and just sit down on my rusty dusty and wait for somebody to wait on me hand and foot. They saw that I wasn't afraid to work. Gaining respect was hard, but now that I'm 27, soon to be 28, I think I finally got that respect.

Q. What are some of the good times you have shared as a family?

P. The dance contest and the dance challenges. I'm big on tradition. I've always wanted a huge family and instantly, I got one. We always ate together—Dad was served first—all of those old, traditional, respectful things. That's what I enjoyed the most.

Q. Now you are married. What is it like bringing your husband into the family?

P. At age 27, this is my second marriage. I knew the type of husband I needed to have for what God has for me to do in this family. I know that I was as much a part of this family as anybody. So, I had to have someone that would fit. And even though *fit* is just a three-letter word, it means so much. He had to fit. He had to first understand my role in this family, and I knew that I had to marry someone that would not take me away from my family. I had to marry someone where I would not lose Penni again. If I lost Penni again, I could not go any further in fulfilling the family vision. It was amazing to find the love of my life. He found me in church running with the vision, and he was running with the vision

The one thing I took with me into my marriage is that the day I said "I do" was the day that his children could come and live with us.

too. Now we're two busy bees running with the vision. It's been awesome and exciting.

He hasn't experienced a Houpe family vacation yet, but he has certainly experienced the family; spending time with Dad and Mom; growing in our marriage; growing in our faith together. It's like we're starting out fresh. We're two kids being molded by parents, Pastor and Mrs. Houpe (Mom and Dad). They're molding us and shaping us. As much as we want to live separate lives, they have so much to offer us. They do not know that just talking to us has made our marriage so much stronger. I thank God for my husband.

Q. If you have to give advice to someone entering into a blended family, what would that be?

P. My husband has two daughters. I am in a blended family. I would say, just be open. The one thing I took with me into my marriage is that the day I said "I do" was the day that his children could come and live with us. You have to be open. You have to be aware of the children. You can't live life as if they're not there and you are just paying child support. Children are not a fantasy, and there is a real possibility that one day they could come to live with you.

EPILOGUE

EPILOGUE

Thank you for allowing us to share our journey toward becoming one family with you and your family. Our prayer is that we have been a light of hope for you as you take your own personal journey with your blended family. The fact that you have journeyed with us has brought tremendous joy to our hearts. We hope you have found some peace and comfort in knowing there are people going through some of the same challenges that you are currently experiencing.

Our attempt was never to present to you a clinical approach to rearing children in a blended family. We are not professionals in that field. We have completely and totally relied on the greatest Physician of them all. We have come to find that His prescription brings a permanent cure for the hurts and pains that manifest in a blended family.

Remember to trust God with your blended family and stay with Him as He leads you on your journey to becoming one.

Our journey does not end here, but we must stop and return to our family. Jonathan is now ten years old and still needs his parents. Christa is entering her senior year of high school, while Darell, Benjamin, and Justin are finding their purpose in pursuing their careers. We must be there to celebrate with them, encourage them, and give them advice when asked. Stephen and Penni are each married with their own blended families. We are now grandparents as part of our children's blended families and are witnessing the next generation of blending. Here we go again! More steps to take to bring blended families together! Remember, as you walk the road toward becoming one family, there is *hope!*

Donna and I would love to hear from you and continue to pray with you as you take your journey. Perhaps if the Lord permits, our paths will cross and we will meet along the way. Please share with us your personal experiences as you bring your blended family together. Near the end of this book you will find information on how to contact us. Remember to trust God with your blended family and stay with Him as He leads you on your journey to becoming one.

May God bless you and your family!

Steve and Donna

APPENDIX

Appendix

The following are a few paths that you may or may not take during your journey toward becoming one family. These are drawn from the experiences of others who, like you and us, are still allowing God to blend their families.

To the Stepmother: Detours to Watch Out For

1. Be prepared for the extended family to refer to your husband's former spouse if she was favored by them. Choose your times to leave the room. If you come to this path, walk it like the godly woman you are.

2. Prepare to feel a bit of tension between you and the stepdaughter as you both initially vie for a place in your husband's heart. The stepdaughter may fight with words and stares and may try to breed confusion and force Daddy to choose between you and her. Remember, you are not the child in this situation, and tantrums are not necessary. Over time,

take control of your house and allow your new daughter to adjust. Remain the mature adult, and trust your husband to make room for both of you in his heart.

3. Be sensitive and careful if it appears that your in-laws are causing division between you and your spouse. This activity may be indicated by remarks from the grandchildren, such as, "Does she cook his meals like Momma does?"

    Kill all forms of division immediately and respond like the godly woman that you are. You might respond by saying, "No, I am not trying to be his Momma, because Momma raised a boy and I married a man. Therefore, we are adjusting to every facet of marriage as we allow God to help us blend this family."

4. Be prepared that the ex-spouse may express that she knows your husband better than you do, and she may become quite descriptive. Your response never needs to be provoking because, after all, you have the ring on your finger and the man by your side. Enough said!

5. Do not be surprised if each child's adjustment to you occurs at different times. Be alert for this. It is merely a reflection of the decision of each of their hearts. You cannot predict or time their

adjustments. However, your consistent love, attention, prayers, and patience for each of them will make their periods of adjustment easier. Accept them where they are, and trust God.

TO THE STEPFATHER: DETOURS TO WATCH OUT FOR

1. Prepare for your wife's son to be very skeptical of you initially. His love for his mother is very strong, and the older he is, the more you may sense some resistance. Here, love and patience are the keys, but allow the child proper time to adjust. Respect for each child's feelings is always necessary when blending a family. Godly wisdom is truly needed in this case. Your spouse will never forgive you if she finds herself losing her son or daughter. Remember, she did not marry you to lose her children. Take each path as you encounter it. Recognize the resistance when it shows up and get wisdom from God to address it. You can find your way along this path through the woods and make it back into the sunshine.

2. The day or night may come when any one of the children may choose to live with their biological father. If you have led your home in a godly manner and based your decisions on godly principles, do not feel slighted by this demand.

Children may choose the option of living in the secondary home merely because of the liberties there. They may not like your current home structure. At this time the decision of you and your spouse is crucial for the well-being of the remaining children who are watching. The two of you will also need to discuss the boundaries by which the child choosing to leave may reenter your home and the rules for that child. Your responsibility as the head of your house is to maintain order and stability for all parties involved. Take this path when you come to it. But remember, take the path and stay on it until you come out on the other side.

Taking the 'Toll Road' for the Stepmother or Stepfather

There is no escape plan to avoid the difficulties of the blended family. Parenting takes tremendous maturity, but to become a godly parent takes spiritual maturity. There will be some battles along the road to becoming one family. Our advice is to pay the toll and take the road.

1. At times, the biological children of your spouse may take a trip down memory lane. These stories will more than likely include the ex-spouse. The memories may be of a family vacation, a birthday

party, a reunion, or some other happy occasion celebrated before your time. You and the children from your previous union may feel totally left out and unable to join in with this journey of memories. There may be nowhere to run to, and you may be feeling really alone in this conversation, with nothing to contribute. You can choose to say something or to say nothing. You may choose to allow the children to share their memories about their life with your spouse before you came on the scene. Interruptions by you or the children from your union may delay the healing process. Remember: When you allow each of the children to hold on to their memories, you open the door for them to heal. Pay the toll and take this road.

2. On occasion you might miss a birthday or some other special day or forget to pick up something for one of the children. Your spouse may become very upset and blame you for ruining the event. Your best response would be to just admit that you forgot and apologize. If your intentions were pure and you genuinely forgot, in time you will come to the exit from this road. However, if you did this on purpose and tried to hurt either your spouse or the child, you are on your

"If the enemy can steal your agreement, he can steal your increase."

own. Whatever the repercussions, pay the toll to reach the goal!

DEALING WITH THE "ROAD CLOSED" SIGNS

A "road closed" sign appears in a union when the husband and wife come to a stand-off concerning a particular issue that affects the family. We ran into several closed roads in our union, and you may also. A road-closed barrier may appear in situations such as the following:

1. You must decide whether to buy a car for the one who has just turned sixteen. The child has not done well in school, but the father insists upon this birthday present for "daddy's little girl."

2. One of the children did not complete all assigned chores or did poorly in school, but still has the privilege of watching a movie. You and your spouse are in complete disagreement concerning the action taken.

Closed roads can manifest in any union, both in a blended family like ours and in a traditional family. The key here is to avoid a stand-off where the two of you are on opposing sides. Instead, do your best to agree on the direction the family should take. The one solution to this problem is the Word of God. Following it will settle the family. Let God's Word and His promises remove the road-closed sign and help you both make it to your destination of becoming one family. If the Word of God is not the foundation for your union and the basis for your decisions, you will encounter many closed roads as you journey together. Remember, "If the enemy can steal your agreement, he can steal your increase." Allow God to have the final say and you will reach the end of this road!

The "Toll-Free Road" for Both the Stepmother and Stepfather

This is a special situation that might come up when the ex-spouse has a history of making empty promises to the children. These promises might include something like the following: "I have a special gift for you under the Christmas tree, and you will get it when you come over." "I will definitely make it to your game" (concert, dance recital, spring festival, karate competition, and so forth).

You are sure that the ex-spouse is merely making empty promises and will not follow through on the gift or show up for any of the above-mentioned events. The children have high expectations and are completely disappointed when the ex-spouse gives his or her usual excuse for not keeping the promise.

Prepare to pick your child's heart up off the floor, and do not feel slighted that your child has not noticed that you have not missed any school function or failed to give any promised gift. Trust us—in time each child will understand and the empty promises will get old.

This road is toll-free simply because you've earned it. Take the road and love the child through the whole ordeal. In time, that child will take the road with you!

FAMILY PRAYERS

Family Prayers
Prayer for Blending a Family

Father, in the Name of Jesus, we admonish You with our petitions, prayers, and intercessions for wisdom in blending our family. We acknowledge that only You know what is best for each of us. We commit ourselves to pray about every concern and care that may arise. We willingly cast them all upon You. Bless us with divine direction. Teach us how to pray—how to settle ourselves and listen for Your wisdom in what to pray about. Thank You, Father, that we can partner with You as we blend our families into one union in Christ Jesus.

Thank You for the precious gift of our children. We lift them up to You. You know what is best for them and what they need. We thank You for godly counsel and assistance as we train them to be positive, obedient, and fulfilled in this family and in life. Bless them to feel loved, accepted, and free to share their concerns and hurts with us as their parents.

We pray that Your will shall continuously be done in each of our lives. We desire that our family bring glory and honor to You. Amen.

SCRIPTURE REFERENCES

1 Timothy 2:1

Ephesians 1:17

1 Peter 5:7

Psalm 127:3

Luke 11:1

Family Prayers
Walking in Forgiveness

Father, in the Name of Jesus, we desire to never walk in offense, but to continuously forgive, forget, and walk in love. Heal us of the hurts and emotional scars of the past. Loose us to walk in total victory in this area of our lives.

Lord Jesus, we decree that we have been crucified with You, and we accept that You live in us. We thank You for the sacrifice that You made on the cross for our sins. We choose to forgive because we don't want the penalty You paid for our sins to have been in vain.

As new beings in Christ Jesus, we cloak ourselves in the garments of praise, thanksgiving, and victory over the old man of unforgiveness, anger, and strife. We trust in You and lean upon Your understanding and not ours.

We confess that our blended family walks in total victory because of our Christ-like nature of love. As a family we know that forgiving is a choice that brings life, whereas not forgiving ushers in sickness and death. Therefore, we choose the abundant life by walking in total love. We shall forgive, forget, and walk in all the blessings of Abraham. Amen.

SCRIPTURE REFERENCES

Matthew 6:15

Philippians 3:13

1 John 5:4

Hebrews 9:26

Romans 6:6

Galatians 2:20

Family Prayers
Peace in Our Blended Family

Father, we thank You that You have blessed our family with Your peace which surpasses all understanding. It is keeping our hearts and minds through Christ Jesus. Our home is built on a firm, godly foundation of wisdom, love, and understanding. We have the sound mind of Christ, and we dwell in peace and love. We are comforted and secure because You are our hiding place.

Help us trust You at all times. We look to You for guidance and truth as we are transformed into Your likeness.

Scripture References

Philippians 4:7

2 Timothy 2:19

2 Timothy 1:7

Psalm 32:7

Psalm 37:3

Philippians 2:5

Family Prayers
Unity in Our Blended Family

Heavenly Father, our family is confident and secure in You. We know that blending a family is not an easy task. But we know that if we ask anything according to Your will, You hear us, and we know that you will grant our requests. Teach us how to live in complete unity so that our lives are pleasing to You, thereby accomplishing Your plan for us as a family.

Father, we pray that each of us in this blended family will operate in total agreement and harmony. We decree that there will be no dissension or strife among us, nor will we allow anyone else to sow discord into our home.

As members of this family, we will live humbly and patiently, with respect for one another, and in love and peace. We will show compassion and respect for each other's welfare, protection, success, and happiness. We honor, esteem, appreciate, admire, and praise those in our blended family.

Jesus, we thank You that we are striving to become one, just as You and the Father are one. Continue to unite our hearts in the bonds of love and peace. Amen.

SCRIPTURE REFERENCES

1 John 5:14,15

1 Corinthians 1:10

Ephesians 4:3

Matthew 18:19

1 Peter 3:8,9

Psalm 86:11

John 17:2–23

FAMILY PRAYERS
IMPROVING COMMUNICATION
IN THE BLENDED FAMILY

Father, in the Name of Jesus Christ, Son of the Living God, as a blended family we make a commitment to You and to each other to control our tongues. We know that Your Word says that the tongue is a fire. We ask forgiveness for every word that we have ever spoken that was displeasing to You, Father, or that may have offended or hurt members of this family.

We now dedicate our mouths to speak only those things that are edifying, excellent, and correct. Our mouths shall utter only truth because we are the righteousness of God in Christ Jesus. We will guard our hearts and our communication with all diligence. We refuse to give the enemy any place in us. We will let no foul or polluting communication, nor evil words, come out of our mouths, but we will speak only that which is good and beneficial to the spiritual well-being of our family.

Our communication shall be with sound words of faith, power, sincere love, and life that shall produce

good things in our lives and the lives of others, in Jesus'
Name. Amen.

Scripture References

James 3:6

Proverbs 8:6,7

2 Corinthians 5:21

Proverbs 4:23

Proverbs 21:23

Ephesians 4:27–29

James 1:6

John 6:63

Colossians 3:16

FAMILY PRAYERS
PRAYER BY A CHILD
IN A BLENDED FAMILY

Father, in the Name of Jesus, I give You honor, praise, and thanks for my biological parents and for my stepparents. I pray for each household that I am a part of. I have been hurt and confused by my biological parents not being together, but I now cast those cares on You, Lord. I release all hurt, bitterness, resentment, jealousy, and disappointments to You. I know that You will continue to keep me in Your care. Anoint me with Your healing power, wherever it is needed.

Heavenly Father, I commit myself to pray daily that I will be calm, loving, obedient, and grateful for my parents and my home. Thank You for the love, guidance, and direction that my parents have provided for me. Forgive me for all the times I did not honor them as I should have. Bless me to know Your will and purpose for my life. Teach me the way that I should go, and guide me. Bless me to love and serve You all the days of my life. Amen.

SCRIPTURE REFERENCES

Psalm 55:22

Romans 12:16–18

Romans 12:10

Ephesians 4:31,32

Psalm 32:8

Philippians 4:6

Jeremiah 29:11

Prayer of Salvation

God loves you—no matter who you are, no matter what your past. God loves you so much that He gave His one and only begotten Son for you. The Bible tells us that "...whoever believes in him shall not perish but have eternal life" (John 3:16 NIV). Jesus laid down His life and rose again so that we could spend eternity with Him in heaven and experience His absolute best on earth. If you would like to receive Jesus into your life, say the following prayer out loud and mean it from your heart.

Heavenly Father, I come to You admitting that I am a sinner. Right now, I choose to turn away from sin, and I ask You to cleanse me of all unrighteousness. I believe that Your Son, Jesus, died on the cross to take away my sins. I also believe that He rose again from the dead so that I might be forgiven of my sins and made righteous through faith in Him. I call upon the Name of Jesus Christ to be the Savior and Lord of my life. Jesus, I choose to follow You and ask that You fill me with the power of the Holy Spirit. I declare that right now I am a child of God. I am free from sin and full of the righteousness of God. I am saved in Jesus' Name. Amen.

If you prayed this prayer to receive Jesus Christ as your Savior for the first time, please contact us on the Web at **www.harrisonhouse.com** to receive a free book.

Or you may write to us at

Harrison House
P.O. Box 35035
Tulsa, Oklahoma 74153

What Others Have to Say About *Becoming One Family*

Becoming One Family is truly a help for "blended" families. Steve and Donna Houpe use biblical principles to show you how to deal with challenges that are a part of the "blended" family.

They show you the importance of getting God involved in the plans and visions for the family. They give you examples from their own experiences of how to love and enjoy each other's children as if they were from their own loins, as well as how to deal with the external parents in love. Steve and Donna are very candid and honest about some of the mistakes they made and how they easily corrected them. Most importantly of all, they knew that they must forgive and forget the past, and live this overcoming and victorious life that Jesus Christ made possible for them.

Finally, I love the way they let each child share out of the honesty of their hearts what living in the "blended" family was like to each of them. As a pastor's wife and minister, I believe every pastor and counselor should read this book. It can be a help and blessing to counseling those who are entering second marriages. I highly recommend this book. It is enjoyable and an easy read.

Dr. Betty R. Price
Crenshaw Christian Center
Ever Increasing Faith Ministries
Los Angeles, CA

Donna and Steve have experience in bringing two families together, and they know what it takes! Their book of revelation plus experience and faithfulness will be a blessing to you in revealing the will of God and how God will truly keep you as you trust Him.

I pastored Donna for many years. She is a wonderful young woman, loves God, and highly respects authority.

My friend, this book is not just about a blended family, but there are enough instructions and directions to set any family free. It is an ideal book for those who are thinking about entering into a marriage relationship. I believe that in reading this book you will find many solutions for trouble in marriage. To my son and daughter, Steve and Donna Houpe, I am very proud of you. You have done a splendid job with this book. This book is a must for every family!

Dr. Leroy Thompson, Pastor
Word of Life Christian Center
Baton Rouge, LA

This book is a gift to the Body of Christ because it gives sensible methods for practicing the fruit of the Spirit in a blended family! God's grace is sufficient and His plans for you are for good, and the Holy Spirit is present to help you and your children fulfill your destinies.

In their book *Becoming One Family,* Dr. Steve Houpe and his wife, Donna, give insight and practical methods on how to bring two families together.

They have developed precise and practical tools for developing healthy relationships with God and with one another. This writing grew out of their own experiences as they struggled and sought God for answers. Their lives have proven that there is *hope!*

Other people talk about breaking generational curses; the Houpes not only prayed but put into practice godly principles that are changing the course of generations to come. Regardless of the past, you can overcome the guilt and shame of broken relationships, develop good communication skills, and determine to live together in obedience to God—forgiven and forgiving.

Healthy relationships do not just happen; they must be developed and maintained. I urge you to pray the prayers and apply the family exercises at the end of each chapter. With God, all things are possible.

Germaine Copeland, Founder
Word Ministries
*Author of **Prayers That Avail Much** Book Series*
Good Hope, GA

Becoming One Family is a dynamic piece of art, built on the foundational principle of Love. The book is best illustrated by the word *pattern*. A pattern is an individual, entity, or unit worthy of duplication. This book is a pioneering model for hope in our current generation to follow in this chaotic world.

This is a must-read book, based on the revelation that the family structure has evolved into a blending. This revelational pattern is truly birthed with a pure heart out of prayer and consecration, ushering in a new technique for our future generations.

Willie Clinkscales
Director of Change International Missions
Creflo Dollar Ministries
Atlanta, GA

Becoming One Family is not only a must-read for blended families, but it is also an excellent resource for anyone who is in the business of helping people. My wife and I are a traditional family and have not personally had to deal with the complex issues of a blended family. However, as a pastor, I had to face the reality that an overwhelming majority of my congregation were daily confronting the issues of ex-spouses, stepchildren, child support, and custody battles. Most of them were not thriving through it. This book has given me the insight I need to more effectively minister to the needs of my congregation.

As a "surrogate" son of Steve and Donna Houpe, I have personally witnessed many of their family challenges and have watched them lead their special family to a place of peace and success. Every page of this book is filled with the truth, their sincerity, and wisdom that only comes from God. I believe it is a vital read for everyone directly or indirectly touched by a blended family.

Dr. Dexter L. Howard, Senior Pastor
Life Harvester Church
Fayetteville, AR

Society inflicts weariness and great pressure on individuals, both single and married. Thus, many individuals often feel a great desire and tremendous need just to be connected with another person who they hope will help them to satisfy the longing in their hearts and fill the emptiness of their souls. Sadly, they fail to realize that those whom they attract are often without fulfilled purpose within their own lives. *Becoming One Family* can be a breath of fresh air for the discouraged and disheartened, for believers and nonbelievers alike, who feel trapped in a mundane and mediocre existence.

Dr. Steve and Mrs. Donna Houpe's insight in this book is the perfect prescription to inject new energy and hope into fatigued hearts. The wisdom they share is sure to infuse fresh excitement and meaning into ordinary lives, as well as lift readers into higher realms of realized potential and fulfillment of God's purpose in their lives.

Dr. James C. Hash, Sr., Pastor
St. Peter's Church and World Outreach Center
Winston-Salem, NC

This is a must-read book for anyone who is in a blended family, who knows someone in a blended family, or who will one day face a similar situation. Pastor and Mrs. Donna Houpe open their lives and the lives of their children to show that there is hope and help for the blended family. This book is a testimony that if God can do it for them, He can and will also do it for you.

Pastor Dewayne Freeman
Spirit of Faith Christian Center
Baltimore, MD

Becoming One Family is an astonishing book. It is not just for the blended family; it is a must-read for anyone embarking upon marriage and parenthood. It encompasses the totality of family—ministering to the husband, wife, and children. The comments and suggestions from Dr. Houpe, his wife, and their children are extremely useful and have proven to help prevent several challenges that arise within the family. This book will afford you the opportunity to converge with an anointed man and woman of God as they open their lives and share their personal experiences with you.

Dr. Cassaundra Singleton
Harvest Church
Kansas City, MO

Endnotes

Chapter 1: Will Your Family Prosper or Perish?

[1] Victoria Neufeldt and David B. Guralnik, eds., *Webster's New World College Dictionary, Third Edition* (New York: Simon & Schuster, 1996).

Chapter 3: Getting a Vision for My Family

[1] Larson, J. (1992). *Understanding Stepfamilies,* American Demographics, 14, 360.

Chapter 4: Where Did It Go Wrong?

[1] CDC Monitoring the Nation's Health; "Cohabitation, Marriage, Divorce, and Remarriage in the United States;" Vital and Health Statistics; Series 23, Number 22; July 2002, Dept. of Health and Human Services; Centers for Disease Control and Prevention; National Center for Health Statistics.

About the Authors
Dr. Steve Houpe

Dr. Steve Houpe is the founder and Senior Pastor of Harvest Church in Kansas City, Missouri. It is one of the fastest growing multi-cultural, interdenominational, cutting edge ministries in the Midwest. Dr. Houpe and his lovely wife, Donna, are the parents of six children.

During more than twenty years of ministry, Dr. Houpe has established:

- Faith Academy—a school to educate children in a strong Christian environment with an emphasis on academics and raising up leaders to impact generations.
- Covenant Alliance of Ministries (CAM)—a ministerial support to mentor and assist young ministers and ministries.
- Leah's House—a home for unwed teenage mothers who decide to keep their babies.
- Mama Jos—an entrepreneurial venture.

Harvest Church Development Corporation—to carry out a community development plan called Project Destiny, which includes: a senior citizens' retirement center, a 2-story medical professionals building, and a commercial strip mall.

Dr. Houpe has authored a number of books and has the distinction of being the first African-American minister from the state of Missouri to open a session of the United States Congress in prayer.

The anointing on Dr. Houpe's life has touched and changed the lives of many. His various life experiences have enabled him to connect and relate to people from all walks of life. He freely shares his own experiences and provides words of wisdom, hope, and encouragement by ministering the infallible word of God.

DR. DONNA HOUPE

Dr. Donna Leah Houpe is the Executive Administrator of Harvest Church and Faith Academy. She is a Louisianan by birth and holds a Bachelor of Arts degree in Elementary Education from Southern University, graduating Magna Cum Laude. She also received a Master's Degree in Education from Louisiana State University and a Doctorate Degree in Christian Education from Faith Bible College.

Dr. Houpe possesses over twenty-eight years of experience in educating children. She has authored several literary works by way of poetry and inspirational writings. Her ultimate desire is to minister to children through the publication of Christian children stories that God has placed in her heart throughout her life. Dr. Houpe wants every child's purpose and destiny to come to fruition with the plan of God for their lives.

Dr. Houpe's ministry, empowered by the Holy Spirit, has touched married, divorced, and single women all over the nation. She is a strong example of the virtuous Proverbs 31 woman. She is a devoted wife and mother to her loving husband and children. Dr. Donna Houpe is a blessed woman of God, following His plan as she assists her husband in carrying forth the vision that God has ordained for Harvest Church.

To contact Drs. Steve and Donna Houpe, write:
Harvest Church
4300 North Corrington Avenue
Kansas City, MO 64117

Call Toll Free: (877) 787-5777

Or visit them on the Web at:
www.harvestchurchkc.org
www.stevehoupeministries.org

*Please include your prayer requests
and comments when you write.*

Fast. Easy. Convenient.

For the latest Harrison House product information and author news, look no further than your computer. All the details on our powerful, life-changing products are just a click away. New releases, E-mail subscriptions, Podcasts, testimonies, monthly specials—find it all in one place. Visit harrisonhouse.com today!

harrisonhouse